CUTTING COLLEGE COSTS

CUTTING COLLEGE COSTS

JAMES P. DUFFY

BARNES & NOBLE BOOKS

A DIVISION OF HARPER & ROW, PUBLISHERS
New York, Cambridge, Philadelphia, San Francisco
London, Mexico City, São Paulo, Singapore, Sydney

For my mother

FIRST EDITION

Designed by Abigail Sturges

Library of Congress Cataloging-in-Publication Data

Duffy, James P., 1941–
   Cutting college costs.

   Includes index.
   1. College costs—United States.   2. College students—United States—Finance, Personal.   3. Universities and colleges—United States—Directories.   I. Title.
LB2342.D84   1988   378′.38′0973   88-45024
ISBN 0-06-055132-1   88 89 90 91 92 CC/FG 10 9 8 7 6 5 4 3 2 1
ISBN 0-06-463728-X (pbk.) 88 89 90 91 92 CC/FG 10 9 8 7 6 5 4 3 2 1

CONTENTS

ACKNOWLEDGMENTS

Writing a book such as this required the assistance and active cooperation of many people who went out of their way to supply me with information and answer my numerous questions. Without their participation the many pieces of information this book contains would not have been brought together to form this complete work. To all those who helped I here express once again my thanks.

Among those who deserve my appreciation, in no particular order, are: Bonnie Gardner of the American Association of Community and Junior Colleges; Harlan P. Hanson, Director of the Advanced Placement Program of The College Board; Dr. Richard W. Moffitt of Ohio University; Cheryl Corn of Walla Walla (Washington) Community College; Beverly Jacobson of Columbia Basin College, Pasco, Washington; Vice Admiral N. R. Thunman, U.S. Navy; Dr. Harold Markowitz, Jr., of the University of Florida; Gretchen Schuette of Linn-Benton Community College, Albany, Oregon; Major John Sondermann, U.S. Marine Corps; Cynthia N. Johnson of the National Commission for Cooperative Education; Jim Carnett of Orange Coast College, Costa Mesa, California; Celeste Holman of Chemeketa Community College, Salem, Oregon; A. Theresa McNally of the University of California Extension; L. David Allen of the University of Nebraska, Lincoln; Captain E. William Stephenson, Jr., U.S. Air Force; Jane A. Johnson of the Community Colleges of Spokane, Washington; D. Richard Petrizzo of the College of DuPage, Glen Ellyn, Illinois; Glynn Ellen Fischelli of Fordham University; Rita V. Ryerson of the Cooperative Education Association; Hugh McCabe and Chris McCabe for their many contributions; Jeanne Flagg for her enthusiasm; Rosalie Rosenthal for her ideas; Larry Brotmann for his invaluable advice; Nancy Rappa for her special help; Mary Gallagher for a place to work; my wife, Kathy, for her support and hard work in helping to put it all together; and Alexandra, whose smile makes it all worthwhile.

INTRODUCTION

The cost of earning a college degree has skyrocketed during the last decade. Financial aid, mostly in the form of large loans that burden both students and parents for years, are now a fact of life for most families with one or more children in college.

This book is designed to help both students and parents find ways of reducing the costs involved in earning a college degree. The information it contains shows you how to save thousands of dollars in college costs.

It also demonstrates several methods that will help reduce the time it takes to earn a degree from four years to three years or less. These timesaving methods will not only save you money, but they will also advance the student's life by one year or more. That means entering graduate school or embarking on the career the degree was intended to enhance a year earlier. Over the length of the student's career that extra year can result in tens of thousands of dollars in increased earnings.

Stores and libraries from coast to coast stock a large assortment of books on financial aid programs. This book isn't another guide to student loans that increase actual costs through interest payments and at best defer payment over a long period of time.

In the following chapters you will learn about viable alternatives that will realistically reduce your college costs. Some are simple to pursue and require only a bit of imagination, while others are part of formal programs that are primarily intended to help you reduce your costs.

Some of the cost- and time-saving techniques you'll learn about here include the use of alternative methods of earning college credits. They all make use of policies and practices currently in force at hundreds of colleges and universities throughout the country. There's nothing in this book that violates standard practices.

How to Use This Book. Each chapter in this book has been designed to help you in some way. Chapters 1 and 2 discuss the costs involved in earning a college degree and what you should know about the availability of scholarships. All the succeeding chapters deal directly with cost- and time-saving methods.

In Chapter 3 you'll see how valuable it can be to use your imagination and think innovatively about ways to cut your college costs. This chapter includes over a dozen ways to save money or time. Chapter 4 shows you how you can save money by attending two different schools.

In Chapters 5, 6, and 7 you will learn how to use correspondence courses, your own experiences, and proficiency examinations to reduce the time it will take you to earn your degree by one full year and sometimes even as much as two years.

Chapter 8 demonstrates several ways in which you can get a head start on your college education, thereby saving time and money. Chapter 9 shows you how to earn money while attending college and help prepare yourself for your career.

Chapter 10 contains in depth information on college tuition assistance that's available from the U.S. armed services. Some programs not only pay part of your tuition but give you spending money as well.

External degrees are the subject of Chapter 11. These are designed for people who are unable to attend college classes on a regular basis.

Once you've learned about all these methods of cutting your college costs, the Appendix brings it all together for you. The more than 1,500 colleges and universities included in the *College Profiles for Cost Cutters* offer you the opportunity to use many of the time- and money-saving techniques discussed throughout this book. Along with the name and location of each college you will find information on which cost-cutting programs are available.

How much you are able to cut the total cost of your college education depends on several factors; the most important is you and how much effort you are willing to expend. Each of the cost-cutting suggestions you'll find in this book can and should be combined with others to save even more time and money. In fact, a real bargain hunter can make use of almost all of them.

Use what you learn from this book wisely. Learn to "shop" for your education as you would for any purchase of this magnitude. Remember you are an education consumer. As an education consumer your goal should be to receive the best quality education at the lowest possible price.

1

CALCULATING
YOUR COLLEGE COSTS

> Anywhere you go, any way you count it, a college degree costs more money than entering freshmen and their parents think it will. Never mind how many taxpayers and rich alumni kick in. What students are expected to pay comes as a rude shock even to the best-heeled families. For families in more modest circumstances, the costs can be overwhelming.

Caroline Bird made this observation in her book *The Case Against College,* published in 1975, when college costs were less than half of what they are today. The impact of the cost of a college degree on the average family is greater than ever. Today it's vital to a family's financial health to find ways of trimming that cost without sacrificing a good education.

A Major Purchase. At one time it was said that paying for the children's college education was the second largest expenditure for many American families. Purchasing a home was the only greater expense. That evaluation is now out of date for many families. This is especially true if they purchased their home before their current college-bound children graduated from elementary school. For many of these families, college costs represent the biggest purchase they will ever make.

The irony of this major purchase is that many families accept what they are told is the price, then seek ways of paying it. They don't react this way when they're told the price of that new car they're thinking of buying. You can bet they didn't accept the seller's price on the house they live in without some attempt to negotiate a better price. In fact, negotiating a better price is the way most Americans approach every major purchase except one—a college education.

A Buyers' Market. Until recently higher education has been a seller's market. The result has been that the costs of attending a college or university have consistently outstripped the rate of inflation and most other costs encountered by the American family. College education is entering a bright new age that will be dear to consumers' hearts—a buyers' market. Some colleges have recognized this and responded with cost-cutting efforts, such as the decision of Robert Iosue, president of York College in Pennsylvania, to use lower-paid administrative assistants to do the work normally done by a vice-president and an associate dean. This saved the school tens of thousands of dollars.

Colleges and universities are going to have to learn to reduce expenses in areas that don't directly affect the quality of their educational efforts. Voices are now being heard that the total price tag is too high. The cost of attending the most prestigious schools for four years is beginning to outweigh the benefit of the schools' degrees.

Be a Smart Consumer. The cost of earning a college degree has more than doubled in the last *decade.* The question isn't if a college degree is worth the time and expense required; basically it is. The question students and parents should be seeking to answer is, "Can I get the same education at a better price?" In spite of the increasing cost and the fact that an ever-increasing percent of the work force holds a college degree, the education and credentials of a degree are still worth the time, effort, and expense involved. On average, college graduates earn approximately 40 percent more than high school grads. In addition, many companies today require a college degree for all but their most menial positions. It's not a matter of skimping on someone's education; it's a matter of being a smart consumer.

Too often people who are normally smart consumers lose their sense of value when confronted by the price tag of a college. They feel guilty if they respond to that price tag in the same manner as they do to any other price tag: "Let's look for a better deal." There's no reason to feel guilty about looking for ways to cut the cost of your child's or your education. The intelligent education consumer can walk away with the same education and the same degree as the person who accepted the list price offered by the college.

When asked if college is worth the price, U.S. Secretary of Education William Bennett said, "Some are, some aren't." His advice was to "kick the tires and make sure you're getting something. When people are making sacrifices to send their kids to college, they should be sure they're getting their money's worth."

Smart consumers can often find the same product at a better price. The same can be true of a college education. One of those smart consumers is Sarah Leah Whitson. After graduating from a Los Angeles public high school with straight A's she was accepted to Yale, but decided to attend the University of California at Berkeley instead. Why? Ms. Whitson's answer is clear: "The difference between going to Yale and going to Berkeley is the difference between buying designer jeans and buying Levi's. You're getting the same quality but at a much lower cost." That lower cost means a savings of approximately $54,000 over four years.

Why Costs Are So High. Eventually everyone planning to attend college or to send their children to college asks the same question: "Why does college cost so much?" The answer depends on who is asked. Critics such as Secretary Bennett claim, "Some of our colleges and universities charge what the market will bear. And lately they have found that it will bear quite a lot, indeed." Massachusetts Democratic Congressman Chester Atkins charges, "Administrators have used federal support to avoid the kinds of cost controls that just about every other institution in our society has instituted in the past few years."

College administrators reject both charges, claiming that tuition increases are needed to improve faculty salaries, which lagged behind the inflation rate in the 1970s, and to purchase new equipment, such as computers to enhance the quality of the education provided.

Save Time and Money. If a college degree is worth the sacrifice most people must make to earn one for themselves or their children, then they must begin dealing with the price tag. The first thing to do is determine as near as possible what four years at your chosen college is going to cost. What's the sticker price? Then find ways of reducing that price without affecting the quality of the education you are buying.

The following chapters offer opportunities for cutting the costs of earning your college degree. Reducing the cost of a college education isn't a simple task, especially if the reduction you seek is to have substantial impact on your final cost.

Some of the cost-reducing methods in this book are based on the old adage "Time is money." When you're attending college, that should be changed to "Time is a lot of money." Just imagine for a moment how much money you would save if you could earn your degree in three years instead of four. You could save a year's tuition, although a small portion of that saving might be needed to pay additional expenses involved in the way you save the year's time. If you aren't living at home with your parents, you'll save a year's living expense whether you live on campus or off. You will also save all the other expenses involved in attending college, such as food, clothing, travel, and recreation.

Perhaps best of all, reducing your college time from four to three years puts you into the income-producing world one year earlier. You can get a head start on your career.

Determining Your Costs. Whatever the cause of the recent sharp increases in college costs, one thing is certain: attending college is going to cost you a great deal of money. What you need to know is how much. The following steps will help you estimate the price tag you will be asked to pay. This price excludes any scholarships or grants you may be lucky enough to be awarded, and it doesn't take into consideration loans that will help pay your costs now but ultimately increase the cost of your education through interest charges. Our concern at this point is to estimate what your education is going to cost, then find ways you can cut those costs.

Step 1: Select Several Colleges. First decide what criteria you'll use in selecting the colleges to which you will apply. Whatever criteria you use, be sure they're personally important to you. If you can't think of any, a good place to begin is to make a list of the colleges with the highest-rated departments in the field in which you intend to major. A second criteria is whether the colleges on this list offer you opportunities to save money. You can find this out by checking each college on your list against the Appendix in this book, *College Profiles for Cost Cutters.*

Any colleges not included in the appendix and those offering limited opportunities for saving money should be set aside. From here on we'll work only with your short list. Try to get this list down to a manageable number—say, four or five. If your short list contains more than five colleges, break it down into two sublists. Follow these steps for each sublist. Then combine the leading candidates from each sublist to form your final list. It will be like a play-off for the winning college on each list. The colleges you place on this final list should have highly rated departments in your field of study and offer their students cost-cutting opportunities.

Step 2: Find Their Costs. Since we want to calculate the true costs you'll have to meet, knowing the tuition charge for a particular college isn't enough. We must also know the other costs, such as room and board, books, supplies, transportation, and miscellaneous expenses.

There are several excellent guides that will give you the current estimates for these expenses at most U.S. colleges and universities. One is *The College Cost Book,* published annually by the College Board; it can be found at most local libraries.

Before going on, let's be sure we understand what these expense categories include.

Tuition and fees. Tuition is what you pay for the education you receive at the college. In addition, extra fees may be charged for use of the school library, for participation in student activities, and for use of other student services the college provides.

Room and board. Unless you commute from home to school each day, food and housing are going to add a large chunk to the overall cost of your college education. Some opportunities to save money in this category are found in Chapter 3.

Books and supplies. One thing is certain—you're going to need books, lots of them over the next few years. For years people have been saying students can cut costs in this category by purchasing used books instead of new ones. While it is possible to save some money this way, in truth many college texts are changed frequently, making it likely that last year's edition is now obsolete. In Chapter 3 you'll find some advice on how to save money when purchasing books for college classes.

Besides books, you're going to need pencils, pens, paper, notebooks, and a myriad of other related items that individually don't cost much but can add up over the course of a year.

Transportation. The transportation expenses most colleges report are based on the student traveling to the college at the beginning of the year, making one round trip home during the year, and going home at the end of the year. Your actual transportation expense will increase dramatically if you make additional trips home or your parents visit you at college.

Miscellaneous expenses. This category includes routine expenses such as laundry, meals taken off campus, snacks, medical insurance, entertainment (everyone likes to go to a movie once in a while, dancing, etc.), telephone charges, newspapers and magazines, and many other out-of-pocket expenses.

Other expenses. In this category you should put any expense not covered by the others. This should include necessary expenses because of a handicap, a health requirement, counseling needs, or any unique personal needs.

Step 3: Complete Worksheet 1. Once you've found the cost estimates for the colleges on your short list in one of these guides, enter that information on Worksheet 1, Calculating College Costs, found on page 9. Using figures reported in a recent edition of *The College Cost Book,* we've completed the Worksheet 1 example as a guide (see page 8). When completing Worksheet 1, look realistically at the estimates the colleges provided. Do you expect to travel home more than once during the year? If so, add the additional expense for these trips to your estimates. Ask similar questions about all the expense categories and answer them honestly. If you're not sure about something, it's better to add the additional expense to reduce surprises during the year. A good motto is, "Always budget for the expense." If you don't use the money, you're ahead.

Step 4: Complete Worksheet 2. When Worksheet 1 is completed, we will have a pretty good idea of what the first year will cost you at each of the colleges on your short list.

Unfortunately, we've estimated only the first year. Without using the timesaving methods discussed in this book you're going to be in college for three more years, so let's extend our estimated costs for the full term of your college attendance. The problem is that we don't know how much these costs will increase over the next three years. The College Board recommends using a 6 to 8 percent increase each year. To be on the safe side, avoid surprises, and look at previous performance, let's increase our current estimates by 10 percent per year. Enter the result of these calculations on Worksheet 2, Cost Extension, found on page 11. This has already been done for you on Worksheet 2 (Example), on page 10.

Step 5: Calculate Your Total Cost. When you add the columns across on Worksheet 2 and enter the result in the total column, you'll have a good estimate of just what college is going to cost over the next four years. Barring any changes in your lifestyle or goals that may alter your expenses, this is what you can expect to spend. Now we can find ways to reduce that expense. You can tackle this problem from two angles. First, find ways of reducing your actual financial outlays in each of these expense categories. Second, find ways of reducing the time it will take you to earn your degree. The latter will help you save money in each expense category. This book will help you save both direct expenses and time. Read it carefully and make use of as many time- and money-saving techniques as you can.

Take one final step on Worksheet 2. For each college listed, add the estimated expense for the first three years. Enter this total in the last column on the right. The difference between this amount and the amount in the total column is an estimate of what you can save by reducing the time it takes you to earn your degree by one year.

Worksheet 1 (Example)
CALCULATING COLLEGE COSTS

College Names	Tuition and Fees	Room and Board	Books and Supplies	Transportation	Miscellaneous Expenses	Other Expenses	Totals
Augsburg College	6,830	2,700	300	400	500	—	10,730
Wheelock College	7,816	3,750	300	250	600	—	12,716
Duquesne University	6,270	3,048	250	448	450	—	10,466
Loretto Hts. College	6,794	3,360	350	630	630	—	11,764
Dickinson College	10,285	3,150	320	240	560	—	14,555

Worksheet 1
CALCULATING COLLEGE COSTS

College Names	Tuition and Fees	Room and Board	Books and Supplies	Transportation	Miscellaneous Expenses	Other Expenses	Totals

Worksheet 2 (Example)

COST EXTENSION

College Names	1st Year	2d Year (add 10%)	3d Year (add 10%)	4th Year (add 10%)	Total	First Three Years
Augsburg College	10,730	11,803	12,983	14,282	49,798	35,516
Wheelock College	12,716	13,988	15,386	16,925	59,015	42,090
Duquesne University	10,466	11,513	12,664	13,930	48,573	34,643
Loretto Hts. College	11,764	12,940	14,234	15,658	54,596	38,938
Dickinson College	14,555	16,010	17,612	19,373	67,550	48,177

Worksheet 2
COST EXTENSION

College Names	1st Year	2d Year (add 10%)	3d Year (add 10%)	4th Year (add 10%)	Total	First Three Years

2

THE TRUTH ABOUT SCHOLARSHIPS

The most sought after form of college financial aid is the scholarship. Unfortunately it's also the least understood, especially by parents who think their bright child will be able to qualify for a scholarship that will pay for a substantial portion of their child's college education.

Availability. Perhaps it's the unwarranted publicity received by a small number of scholarship programs, but whatever the reason, many prospective college students and their families believe there are innumerable scholarship funds pouring out money for smart students. Nothing could be further from the truth.

When compared to the number of college students and graduating high school students planning on attending college, the number of scholarships is small indeed. Full scholarships, those that pay all or almost all a student's costs, are especially rare. They're also extremely difficult to win.

Despite this, it would be foolish for any student to ignore the possibility of qualifying for and being awarded a scholarship. Be realistic—don't count on it. If you are one of those lucky students who are awarded a scholarship, it will be financial assistance you hadn't included in your quest to meet the cost of attending college.

Financial Need. Another misconception many parents have about scholarships is that they are based on the student's scholastic abilities. While it is true that some scholarships are strictly academic, most are awarded on a basis of need and not performance. They are combined with the student's other financial aid. This means that many scholarships are based on the parent's ability to demonstrate their level of need, just as they must to qualify for a student loan.

At one time scholarships were awarded by the individuals or

organizations that established and paid for them. The majority are now administered by the financial aid offices of colleges and universities. This change was brought about as part of the movement to open college to everyone regardless of academic performance and ability to pay.

The 1986 Tax Law and Its Effect on Scholarships. Most scholarships are for relatively small amounts of money and are usually part of a student's financial aid package. Of course, the scholarships that everyone wants are the full scholarships. Not only are these few in number, but the benefits have been reduced since the massive tax law overhaul in 1986. The portion of a full scholarship used for tuition, fees, and books remains tax-free, but the portion used for living expenses is taxable income to the student.

Beginning in 1987 a college student could exclude from income reported for federal tax purposes only amounts received as a *qualified scholarship.* According to the Internal Revenue Service a qualified scholarship is any amount received that is used according to the conditions of the scholarship or grant for

- tuition and fees to enroll in or attend an educational institution, or
- fees, books, supplies, and equipment for courses at the educational institution.

Other amounts such as money received for room and board, travel, or miscellaneous expenses are no longer excludable from income, and federal income tax must be paid on them.

The 1986 tax law also provides that all payments for services such as teaching and research must be listed as income even if the services are a condition of receiving the grant and required of all candidates for the degree.

Unused Scholarships. The most widespread myth about scholarships is that thousands of them worth hundreds of thousands or even millions of dollars go unawarded each year. This is simply not true. Remember that every college and university in the country maintains a staff of people, generally known as the financial aid office, which spend an enormous amount of time hunting down every scholarship and grant dollar they can find.

While it's true that occasionally a scholarship is not awarded in a particular year, it's also true that the same scholarship has such stringent rules that only rarely does a student qualify. The rules may require that a student have a particular last name, that his or her ancestors come from a particular village or province of a European country, and that the student plan to spend the rest of his or her life as a missionary in the Himalayas. The chances are great that if you qualify for even an oddball scholarship such as this one, the financial aid office of your college will find it for you.

Where the Money Goes. Let's say you qualify for a scholarship. Don't be surprised if the amount for the award doesn't reduce the amount of money you are required to pay for your education. For example, suppose you are of Italian ancestry, your grandparents having come to America from Calabria, and you are majoring in horticulture. In your quest to find money to pay for your education you hunt through directories of scholarships and find one that was established years ago by an Italian immigrant, also from Calabria, who made his fortune in America in the landscaping business.

As you read the description of the scholarship you find that the rules require recipients to be descendants of people from Calabria and that they major in horticulture. The award is $2,000. Bingo! You know you qualify, and you expect to be able to reduce your family's expenses for your education by $2,000. It doesn't work that way. The $2,000 from the landscaper's scholarship bequest becomes part of the financial aid package the college puts together to pay that portion of your college costs you are not required to pay. The scholarship money does not necessarily reduce the amount of money the financial aid office has determined you must pay.

Scholarship and grant money is available to college students in the millions of dollars, and you should seek to qualify for as much of it as possible, but don't count on this source as a panacea for the burden you and your family will face in paying for a college education.

3
OVER A DOZEN WAYS TO SAVE TIME AND MONEY

The old saying "Time is money" is never more true than when applied to college costs. Here are over a dozen methods to reduce the time spent earning your college degree as well as the costs involved. Some of these suggestions may be familiar, while others will be new. Reading them and finding ways to use them will help you develop a different approach to thinking about college costs.

Thinking Innovatively. Getting yourself to think innovatively isn't as difficult as it may sound. It's a more creative approach to problem solving than most people generally use.

To become an innovative thinker you must develop the ability to look at a problem from a different angle than others do. Take the problem of how in the world you're ever going to be able to pay the huge bill a college will hand you for allowing you to be a student for four years. Most people leave their creative thinking to more artistic endeavors and rely on the good old head-on approach to a problem like this. Instead of looking at the bill and trying to answer the inevitable question "How am I going to pay all that money?" the innovative thinker asks, "How can I reduce the total cost of that bill?"

Negotiate and Shop Around. While it may not always be possible to negotiate down the tuition of your favorite college, it is possible to find ways around some of the charges. Don't hesitate to use the financial aid package offered by one college to squeeze more money out of another. Don't be fooled by the ivy-covered walls and the air of gentility some colleges put on, as they are in the market of selling a product—a college education. They don't want you to go to someone else who is selling the same product, so negotiation is the name of the game.

———

When John Franklin and his parents read through the catalogues John had received from each of the colleges he selected as his top three choices, they were shocked at the costs. John had purposefully avoided the higher-priced colleges because he knew they were completely out of his parent's range, even if they went into hock for the rest of their lives. John's father worked in a small factory for a modest wage, and his mother stayed at home caring for his two younger sisters. John realized his parents weren't able to afford any of the three schools, so he began looking for ways to cut the costs.

The first thing John discovered was that one college charged students on a unit basis, meaning that the tuition for a semester was based on a charge per class taken. John soon found the school offered evening and weekend classes at a discount of 30 percent off the cost of taking the same course during the more popular weekday hours. John reasoned that he was going to be on campus during the evenings and weekends anyway, so why not schedule as many evening and weekend classes as possible. A close reading through the schedule of classes and some quick arithmetic showed John and his parents they could save almost 20 percent of the first semester's costs by John taking as many weekend and evening classes as he could.

———

Supply and Demand. Not long ago colleges and universities could handpick the students they wanted, rejecting all others. Today that situation has changed for many colleges. We're in a buyers' market as witnessed by the number of colleges that are advertising in newspapers and on radio and television for students. Many have become innovative in the programs they offer to attract students. This is especially true when it comes to finding ways of providing financial aid to students who otherwise might not be able to afford to attend college.

Some colleges offer a discount to the sons and daughters of alumni. Others offer low-interest loans to financially needy students. Some pay a headhunter's fee of as much as 10 percent of your tuition if you get another student to enroll. When reviewing a college you are considering for application, you'll have to do some prodding among the people in the admissions department to find out if the college has any unusual student benefits such as those just mentioned that might be applicable to your particular situation. Don't be shy about this. You may find a little-known or -used program that could save you hundreds or even thousands of dollars.

———

Lake Erie College in Painesville, Ohio, made an offer to Carrie and Denise Reed they found hard to refuse. They were offered a 2-for-1 special if both twins attended Lake Erie. The business majors saved themselves and their parents over $24,000 by accepting the offer.

———

Proclaim Your Independence. For the truly desperate there's always the possibility of declaring yourself emancipated. Many colleges set aside grants or other forms of financial aid for emancipated, or independent, students. Some go so far as to waive all tuition charges for such students. While the original intent of many of these programs was to provide an education to students who were orphans or wards of the court, there are so many loopholes that some families have succeeded in "driving" several children through them and reaping great benefits.

Besides these special college programs there is also a benefit to be realized when applying for government-supported financial aid. If the student can substantiate independence from his or her parents, the parents' assets and income are not considered when determining how much aid the student is qualified to receive.

Your ability to pay for your college education is based on your own assets, income, and expenses. Because an independent or self-supporting student generally has greater living expenses than one who lives in the parents' home, or is provided with an allowance by the parents, and the typical independent student's income is much less than the dependent student's parents' income, there is an obviously greater need for financial assistance. There will also be extra expenses if the student has a legal dependent, such as a child, to support.

A few years ago the status of "independent student" was discovered by dependent students who realized the benefits they and their parents could receive if they declared themselves independent. That's when otherwise loving parents began "unloading" their college-age sons and daughters, at least in a legal sense. When the sudden increase in independent students awakened aid officials to what was going on, the rules regarding independent, or self-supporting, students were tightened, but not by much.

Eligibility. The following criteria are used to determine the eligibility for U.S. federal student-aid programs of a student who claims to be independent. Some states use the same criteria as the federal programs, while others are more liberal or, as is usually the case, more restrictive. If you are considering declaring yourself an independent student, be sure to check the rules in the state in which you are going to attend school.

To be an independent student for federal aid, the student must:

- Not have lived in the parent's home for more than six weeks for each of the previous two years.*
- Not be listed as a dependent on the parent's income tax return for the previous two years.*
- Not have received more than $750 in support (including cash, food, and lodging) from the parents during each of the two previous years.*

A student can also be considered independent if he or she meets one or more of the following criteria:

- Be 24 years of age or older by December 31 of the year in which the award is made.
- Has legal dependents other than a spouse.
- Be a veteran of the U.S. Armed Forces.
- Be an orphan or ward of the court.
- Be declared independent by a financial aid official who has documented reasons of unusual circumstances.

Declaring your independence can bring you a long way toward reducing what you or your parents will have to pay for college, but it should be considered carefully and planned for well in advance. If you declare your independence and receive any benefits because of it, such as reduced or free tuition, be careful that your status doesn't change while you are receiving them. If you do something to change your status, such as move into your parent's home, or if they claim you on their income tax, you must report this to the school's financial aid administrator immediately.

Get a Job. This may not sound like new advice, but I'm referring not to just any job, but one with a company that will pay your college tuition. Most large corporations, and an increasing number of smaller ones, are willing to pay at least part of the costs of improving the education of their employees. Some will pay virtually all the costs. According to *CFO Magazine,* reimbursement of college costs "has become one of the most popular optional benefits a company can offer."

---

*In early 1988 Congress was contemplating a change to three years. Students are advised to check with the source of aid for current requirements.

There are some obvious disadvantages to doing this. The major one is that getting an employer to pay for your college education will require you to work, which usually means full-time college is out. On the other hand, if you're not able to afford college yourself, going as a less than full-time student beats not going at all.

Advantages to You. Some of the advantages of going to work for an employer who will pay your college tuition are:

- Someone else pays all or nearly all your tuition.
- You are earning a salary to cover your other living expenses.
- You are gaining valuable work experience.
- If you select your employer properly, you are improving your chances for employment in your chosen field after graduation.

How It Works. Plans vary from company to company, but most fall into two basic categories. Some pay virtually all your tuition and directly related costs such as textbooks and fees. Others pay a predetermined percent of your tuition, but nothing for textbooks and fees. Another difference is that some companies pay for college credit courses of any kind so long as you are pursuing a degree, while others pay only for courses related to your field of work. A third difference is how the bill is paid. Some benefit plans pay the costs in advance. Should you drop out of the course or fail to pass you must reimburse your employer.

The Philadelphia consulting firm of Hay/Huggins surveyed large and mid-sized companies that had reimbursement of college costs as part of their employee benefits package and found over half of them pay the full cost of the employee's tuition; about one-quarter reimburse the employee for a set portion of tuition; and the remaining quarter base the reimbursement on either the employee's grades or the credit hours taken. The survey found that although many companies put a limit on the total reimbursement for college tuition an employee can receive each year (an average of $2,000), others have no such limit.

At one time some companies offered reimbursement for college tuition only to select categories of workers. These were usually top- and middle-level managers, and technical-based employees, such as engineers. The Deficit Reduction Act of 1984 changed that when it made such a discriminatory benefit liable to loss of its tax deductibility.

Most company benefit plans reimburse you after you have completed the semester and presented the benefits administrator with your paid bill. Some employers require you to provide proof that you've met certain criteria, such as a minimum passing grade.

How Companies Benefit. Companies offer reimbursement for college courses as a benefit to encourage present employees to work toward advancing their own education and knowledge. This increases their value to the company and improves their promotion opportunities. It's also a way for companies to help keep highly motivated people. Few offer this as an inducement to prospective employees because they're concerned about potential abuse by those seeking help with their college costs. Although one company representative did tell me:

> Look, I don't care if someone I want to hire decides to accept my offer solely because he or she wants our company to pay for their college education. The way our plan works they have to be employed with us for six months before they become eligible for tuition reimbursement. Then, even if they already have some college credits it's going to take anywhere from three to six years to earn a degree part-time. By the time they've earned their degree, they may have received a promotion or two, taken advantage of some of our other employee benefits, and gotten used to working for us. If we can offer them promotional opportunities that correspond with their new college degree there's a good chance they'll stay with us. On the other hand, we've had a good opportunity to observe this person as an employee and know just what we're getting when they complete college and are looking for a better job.

Here are some examples of how college costs reimbursement programs work:

- Knogo Corporation of Hauppauge, New York, manufactures antitheft devices. As part of its employee benefits package, Knogo will reimburse an employee 100 percent of college tuition, providing the employee earns a grade of at least B. The maximum reimbursement is $1,800 per employee each year.
- Maritz, Inc., of Fenton, Missouri, places no maximum dollar amount on its college reimbursement benefit, believing this might prevent employees from attending the best schools for which they could qualify. Instead, the company reimburses an employee for 75 percent of costs for a maximum of 16 credit hours each year.

Locating a Job. Finding a company that will pay for your college education takes time and effort, but it's time well spent. Since few companies have the attitude of the company rep just quoted, you'll discover it isn't easy to find out exactly what most companies' college reimbursement program is until you're actually employed. Instead of making the most of this benefit, many companies hide it from prospective employees, evidently afraid of hiring people whose only motivation is tuition reimbursement.

The place to start is to make a list of the employers in your area that hire people to work in the field you intend to study. If your area of interest isn't that specific, such as business or accounting, then make a list containing the largest employers in the area, including local facilities of large national or multinational companies.

Visit each company and ask if there are any jobs available. Regardless of the availability of a job for you, most employment offices will require you to complete an application and be interviewed. Don't ask the interviewer directly if the company has a college reimbursement program. Ask to see the company's benefits folder. Many companies publish a complete list of their employee benefits in the form of a folder or brochure. If this doesn't give you the information you want, then ask about the company's educational benefits, such as in-house training programs and college courses. Avoid a direct question about college reimbursement. If all else fails, wait outside at quitting time and ask someone leaving the building if their company pays college tuition costs for employees. If possible, ask several people, since not all employees are interested in, and therefore aware of, this benefit.

The Hay/Huggins survey found that between 5 and 10 percent of employees eligible for college tuition reimbursement as a benefit from their employer actually take advantage of it. The money's out there waiting for you, so go get a job that will pay for your college education.

Get Your Parent a Job at College. Colleges and universities are employers just like most businesses. Unlike most businesses they tend to pay a little less than the prevailing wage for nonfaculty jobs. This handicap is usually balanced by an attractive employee benefits program. At many colleges, especially private ones, a benefit of employment is free tuition for employees and their dependents. In some colleges the tuition isn't free, but it is dramatically reduced.

While it may sound drastic for a parent to quit his or her job to take one at a nearby college so they can take advantage of the free or nearly free tuition benefit, the possibility of doing so should be reviewed carefully. Unless the parent is in a well-paying career job, the move may prove to have other benefits as well. This kind of change is especially beneficial when one wage earner in the family isn't in a career job.

_____

When John and Gina Davis (fictitious names) decided to plan for their children's college education, their two sons were in high school. One was a sophomore, the other a junior. John worked for a large corporation downtown, where he was a middle-level manager. Gina, who had returned to the work force three years earlier, was a secretary at a small marketing firm located a few miles away. The Davises realized they were going to have to go deeply into debt if they were going to be able to send both their sons and their daughter, who was still in elementary school, to college.

One day John was discussing the situation with a friend who taught history at a well-respected private college in the area. The friend told John the school was looking for secretarial help in several departments, and suggested the school's employee benefit of free tuition for employees and their families might help the Davises solve their problem of how to pay for college.

John and Gina talked it over, and Gina applied for the positions. Although the position she accepted paid about $2,000 less than she was earning, both the Davis boys have now graduated from a college they would otherwise not have been able to afford. Does Gina regret changing jobs? "Not really," she says, "I enjoyed working at the marketing firm, but I also like working at the school." Tuition at the college is approximately $3,000 per year per student. During the last six years the Davis sons received educations that would otherwise have cost the family $24,000. That's double Gina's before-taxes income difference between the marketing job and the one at the college, and their daughter starts college next year.

_____

The Davises aren't the only people to take advantage of the opportunities of working at a college to get a free or nearly free education. I know a young woman who earned her associate's degree while she worked at a community college. Although she hadn't taken the job for the educational benefit, she decided to take advantage of it while she was employed by the school. After earning the associate's degree she wanted to go on to a bachelor's degree, but was put off by the expenses involved. On a lark she sent her resume to several colleges in the area, seeking a position similar to the one she held at the community college. Since her experience in financial aid administration was in demand she received two job offers. Both were from colleges offering free tuition to employees and their families. She's now on her way to earning a bachelor's degree. The total cost of her education, including books and other items, has been less than 15 percent of what anyone else would pay for it.

Live Off Campus. Many colleges permit students to live off campus as a means of saving money. If you do decide to find off-campus living quarters, try to combine your living arrangements with some work that will reduce your living expenses even more. For example, you might find a family that's in need of a baby-sitter and is willing to let you live in their guest room in return for your services as a baby-sitter or nanny. If you're handy with tools, you might try offering your services as a handyman or groundskeeper at a nearby estate or country club in return for living quarters.

One family that owns a large home near a private college has been in the habit of renting several of their spare rooms to students. In return for reduced rent one student mows the lawn, picks up the leaves, and shovels the snow; another cooks breakfast and dinner during the week; another does housekeeping chores and the family wash; and still another gives piano lessons to the family's children. Everyone benefits by the arrangement, and most of the students stay with the family for their entire four years.

Depending on the school you attend, and the kind of living arrangements you make, living off campus could save you as much as $2,000 per year.

To learn if the colleges you are interested in attending will permit you to live off campus, check each college's catalogue. If you can't locate any information on this or any other subject, call the college admissions office. When you get your answer, ask where you can find it in writing. Remember what a person tells you over the telephone doesn't constitute college policy. Always get it in writing.

Get a Job on Campus. Campus jobs generally have the advantage of being easy to get to from your last class. If your schedule permits, you might even be able to pick up a few hours' work between classes. A good on-campus job to consider is cafeteria work. Along with the salary, cafeteria jobs usually include the benefit of free meals; so in addition to earning extra money, a cafeteria job can save you $1,000 or more each year in food expenses.

Build Personal Contacts. Many times who you know is as important as what you know; sometimes it's more important. Good relations with faculty and other members of the college staff can be the best source of information on the better-paying campus jobs. They can also supply excellent references to potential employers. Someone with whom you have a good personal contact may be able to help you in a way you never thought of.

———

Linda Malta had an excellent record at the public community college she was about to graduate from. She had high grades, had been active in extracurricular activities including editor of the student newspaper, and was a personable student liked by everyone who came in contact with her. One was a member of the college's financial aid office. When Linda told him she was planning to attend a nearby public four-year college to earn her bachelor's degree, he was surprised. With her grades and record of other activities he knew Linda was sure to be accepted by one of the more highly regarded private colleges in the area. When questioned about this, Linda confessed that she couldn't afford a private college. Although she worked as many evenings and weekends as her school-work permitted, Linda's income barely met her living expenses, and all she had been able to save was $1,000.

The financial aid administrator called his counterpart at a nearby private college and discussed Linda's case. Since the semester had already begun, the private college official knew how many student spaces hadn't been filled. Following a long conversation about Linda, her grades, extracurricular activities, and her SAT scores, the college accepted her. Her junior-year tuition was set at $1,000, with the understanding the school would find financial aid for her remaining year if she maintained her grades.

———

Two things worked in Linda's favor. First was the contact she had with the community college financial aid administrator. He would never have gone out on a limb for her if he hadn't known her and wasn't sure she would meet the private college's expectations, and he believed she deserved the opportunity. The second was the availability of an open student space at the private college. That school's official knew adding Linda to the student body wasn't going to cost the school anything. In return the school received Linda's $1,000 and a student with excellent potential.

Fill an Empty Seat. In New York City's Broadway theater district there's a kiosk that sells tickets to many shows at half-price. The tickets become available a few hours before showtime, when it's obvious that there will be some empty seats in the house for that performance. The theater owners would rather sell the seats at half-price than have them remain empty through a performance. Half a ticket price is better than nothing. The same thing happens at many colleges. As colleges spend more time and money market-ing their services to a declining number of prospective students they have a need to fill all the seats available, even if they have to do so at a discount. Although I don't recommend relying solely on this standby method, you may improve the level of the college you are attending by calling around at the last minute to see what's available. Because most colleges refuse to admit this is part of their practice, doing this on your own may prove less productive than having someone with contacts do it for you. If you've just graduated from high school, perhaps your counselor will help. Of course, the success rate depends on your grades, your relationship to the person you've asked for help, and the need of the colleges he or she calls.

Learn on the Fast Track. Some students are capable of handling a greater work load than is normally required in a college semester. Recognizing this, many colleges offer such students the opportunity to earn their degrees in less than four years, providing they can do the work.

Accelerated degree programs make it possible to reduce the time required to earn a bachelor's degree from four to three years. Besides the savings on room and board, the primary advantage to the student is graduation from college one year earlier. This enables you to either enter graduate school or the work force a year earlier than your classmates. Just imagine how much that extra year can be worth over the course of your career.

How Accelerated Degree Programs Work. While some colleges refer to this approach as a three-year degree program and others as an accelerated degree program, they all operate in generally the same way. The student must take the initiative and ask for permission to use an accelerated program. This permission is generally granted by a dean. Students are allowed to accelerate their learning on an individual basis. The decision to permit a student to accelerate is usually based on his or her grades. An accelerated learning program can be a great time- and expense-saving device. Most students who make use of this approach earn their degree after only three years in college.

To learn which colleges offer accelerated degree programs see the Appendix, *College Profiles for Cost Cutters.*

Pay in Advance. This isn't an option for everyone, but it's one that can save you thousands of dollars. Known by different names at the schools that offer them, these plans generally set the tuition and sometimes other charges for a student's four years at the rate in effect when the student enters college, providing the four years' charges can be paid in advance.

One of the earliest of these plans was introduced in 1979 by Washington University in St. Louis. Called the Tuition Stabilization Plan, it froze tuition charges for incoming freshmen who were able to pay for the entire four years at the time they were admitted.

In 1985 Washington University began the Cost Stabilization Plan that froze other charges, such as room and board, at the freshman-year rate in return for prepaying the four years. To help families that can't afford to pay the total all at once, the university permits parents to apply for unsecured loans from the school at favorable rates. The flexible repayment programs can run from four to ten years, starting one month after the loan is made. Interest charges on these loans for the 1988–89 school year were 9.2 percent.

To learn which colleges offer guaranteed tuition programs see the Appendix, *College Profiles for Cost Cutters*.

Change Your State. Almost 80 percent of all college students attend public institutions. That's a radical change from only thirty years ago when the student population was about evenly divided between public and private colleges and universities. The primary reason for this, besides the improved academic standing of many public colleges, is the cost. A degree earned at a publicly supported college could end up costing one-quarter what the identical degree would cost at a private institution, provided you are a resident of the state in which the school is located.

Dual Tuition. Since state-supported colleges are paid for by state taxpayers, the universal feeling is that residents of the state should benefit most from the taxpayers' benevolence. As a result, state-sponsored colleges and universities have a dual tuition policy. The lower taxpayer-subsidized tuition is charged to students who are state residents; a higher tuition, often as much as triple the resident rate, is charged to students from out of state. Some states take part in cooperative programs that permit students from one state to enroll in a public college in another state at the resident tuition. States having such arrangements include Georgia–Tennessee, Kentucky–Mississippi, Oregon–Washington, and Minnesota–South Dakota. Usually the arrangement is limited to specific majors or certain schools.

Another interstate program is the Western Undergraduate Exchange. Under the plan students from any one of ten Western states can enroll in almost any two- or four-year public college in the other nine states and pay only 50 percent more in tuition than residents of that state do. In some states this means a student can save up to half of the out-of-state tuition normally charged. The states in the program are Alaska, Colorado, Hawaii, Idaho, Montana, Nevada, New Mexico, North Dakota, Utah, and Wyoming. For further details contact the Western Interstate Commission for Higher Education, Boulder, Colorado.

So, what do you do if you can't find a state college or university in your home state that has the program you want, or for whatever reason you decide you must attend a certain public university in another state?

First, you must learn what the residency requirement is. In many states you must be a resident for one year to qualify for the resident tuition. You should be able to find this out from the admissions office of the college you are determined to attend. Next, ask what proof is required to substantiate your claim of residency. Many times a driver's license, bank account, rent bill, or similar evidence of residency is needed.

Armed with this knowledge, and determined to save money by not paying the out-of-state tuition, establish your new residency. If you know someone living in the state, such as a friend or relative, your new residency won't cost you anything. If all else fails, rent a furnished room somewhere within the state long enough to meet the residency requirement. You can arrange to have your new landlord forward your mail to you. Establishing a residency like this could save you thousands of dollars when you attend the school of your choice.

Some states alter their residency requirements as the need arises. Florida, in need of highly educated young people to manage its fledgling high-tech industry, will waive out-of-state charges for second-year students who say they intend to live in Florida after graduation. If you do not wish to establish a second residency, then ask the college office if the residency requirement can be met by living on or off campus during your freshman year. Many public colleges don't advertise the fact out-of-state students can qualify for residency tuition charges after their first year in the college, even if they've lived on campus. If living on campus doesn't apply toward the residency requirement, then by all means take advantage of the normal cost savings by living off campus, get a new driver's license, and apply for a change in your status to in-state student.

Become a Commuter. If you're determined to save money on your college education, then by all means look closely at the schools located within commuting distance from your home. Living at home and attending college does have its disadvantages, but saving the living expenses, telephone bills for calls home, the travel expenses for you and for your parents when they visit you, all may make it possible for you to attend a college that might otherwise be beyond your means. Commuting to college every day could save you about $2,000 a year, depending on the room and board charges of the school you're attending.

Avoid the College Bookstore. Two things work against you when you try to save money on the purchase of textbooks. First is the frequency at which textbooks are revised and new editions issued. If your professor insists you use this year's edition for his or her class, then last year's edition, which you can get for less than half-price at a nearby used-book store, will not be acceptable.

This practice of frequent editions has led to charges that it is primarily aimed at maintaining sales and royalties. After all, publishers and authors—the latter sometimes being the same people teaching the class—can't make any money on students who buy used books.

The second thing that works against saving money on books is the timing of the announcement of what books are to be used. Many times students have less than a week to acquire the books they need. Of course, the books are readily available at the college bookstore because the store was told months ago what books were going to be used so they could stock them. They're usually sold at a much higher price than you would pay anywhere else.

The college bookstore, if privately operated, is generally not to blame for the high prices. Besides paying the college rent, the store's owners may also have to pay a percent of their sales to the college. The result is the store must increase the prices of its inventory just to make a profit. This means books cost students more money.

When you learn what books you'll need, check the prices at the college bookstore, and then ask to see the latest copy of *Books in Print.* This multivolume publication lists all books currently in print by title, author, and subject. Locate the entries for the books you need. Along with the author and title, each entry tells you the retail price of the book. This will probably be less than the college bookstore price. Many times a book is published in two editions: one for regular bookstores with the price printed on it, and one for college bookstores without the price on it. This is especially true of the larger (trade) paperbacks. You can verify this at almost any used-book store just by noting the presence or absence of a printed price on similar books.

When you find the book is available in a lower-priced regular edition, rush to the nearest full-service bookstore. If the book isn't in stock, ask how quickly it can be obtained for you. With today's computerized inventory systems most books can be gotten from a distributor or wholesaler within days. This service might carry a small charge, but the book will cost substantially less than the over-priced edition at the college bookstore, and you will be fighting a system that causes students to pay more than necessary for the books they need.

Use the Library. Still on the subject of textbooks, don't overlook the college library or even a local library nearby. This may sound obvious, but it's surprising how many students forget about looking for a book in the library and rush out to the bookstore when they need a book. Your college library is designed to help facilitate your studies. Most have places where books that can't be taken on loan can be read and studied in peace and quiet. The library will be especially helpful by providing those books that have to be read for the course but are not required for the full semester. Remember, the library first, then pursue the cheapest price for a book you must purchase.

Combine Your Degrees. If you intend to go on to earn an advanced degree after you've been awarded a baccalaureate, then you should seriously consider taking graduate courses at the same time you take undergraduate courses. This means more work for you each semester that you're able to do so, but it can result in cutting the time it takes to earn both degrees by at least a year. Many colleges will permit students with high grades to increase their work load by adding graduate courses that earn them credits toward an advanced degree.

4

THE DUAL SCHOOL PLAN

Before accepting President Reagan's appointment as permanent U.S. representative to the United Nations, Jeane Kirkpatrick was Leavey professor of political science at Georgetown University and resident scholar at the American Enterprise Institute for Public Policy Research.

Mrs. Kirkpatrick earned her M.A. and Ph.D. from Columbia University after having received her baccalaureate from Barnard College. What the diploma from Barnard doesn't tell the observer, but Mrs. Kirkpatrick gladly will, is that a portion of the credits required for the Barnard degree were earned at a community college. In fact, Jeane J. Kirkpatrick is a proud graduate of a two-year community college, as are Calvin Klein, O. J. Simpson, Jim Lehrer, Sam Shepard, and Pete Rozelle.

One way to cut your college costs and be sure of receiving a quality education is to attend a community or junior college for two years, then transfer to a four-year college or university for the second two years. As you will see, there are numerous benefits, aside from the cost savings, you can accrue by taking this route.

America's community and junior colleges can be found in almost every county in the United States. There are over 1,200 of them offering educational programs at over 1,500 campuses. While the overwhelming majority of these colleges are state supported, a small number operate as private nonprofit schools. Seventy-one are church-related institutions and 14 are independent for-profit colleges. For the sake of convenience we'll use the term *community college* to include both community and junior colleges.

What Is a Community College? Just as the name implies, these are community-based colleges that provide higher education opportunities to individuals without the need to travel long distances or live in a dormitory. They award associate's degrees, which usually require one-half the number of credits needed for a bachelor's degree.

Most community colleges maintain strong ties with local high schools and businesses in the community. This helps them provide a wider variety of services to their students than many universities can. These include job placement, job-specific training, and developmental education programs in reading, writing, and math for those students who aren't ready for successful completion of college academic programs.

In many areas of the country, community colleges serve as cultural centers. They often provide live theater, classical music, and art and dance events for the community-at-large.

Two Types of Education. Community colleges offer two types of education. For the student planning to go on to earn a bachelor's degree, the education is similar to that offered during the first two years at a four-year college or university. Vocation-oriented students will find community colleges provide valuable training in a wide variety of trades. Since the majority of community college students are part-time, the college schedules tend to be much more flexible than four-year colleges.

A Quality Education. At one time people thought of community colleges as primarily for those unable to get into a four-year college. This is no longer the case. Although some academics at four-year colleges and universities look down their noses at their local brethren, most recognize community colleges for what they have become: institutions of higher learning that provide a quality education for those entering the work force, and excellent preparation for those seeking a higher degree.

In the words of one community college official: "The quality of education [at a community college] is normally far superior to the first two years at a university because all of the community college faculty are fully degreed or otherwise prepared for their assignments."

The scourge of many college students during their freshman and sophomore years at some four-year institutions are the packed lecture halls and classes taught by graduate students instead of professors. These two conditions are not found at community colleges. With a national student/faculty ratio of 20:1 since 1980, community colleges offer their students closer attention than they'll find at most four-year colleges.

———

Although he was accepted by both UCLA and the University of California at Santa Barbara, Kregg Strehorn chose a community college, Orange Coast College. One reason was to save money that he could apply to his junior and senior years at a four-year college. Kregg found "the quality of the teachers on this campus is unbelievable. I have friends who went straight from high school to major four-year schools. They are sitting in lecture classes with 600 other people, and their professors, quite frankly, don't care if they attend classes or not. That's not the situation here at Coast. Teachers here really care about you. If you've got a problem, they'll sit down and talk to you about it. You're not just a number here."

———

Kregg's experience is not unique. Graduate after graduate of community colleges praise the quality of the education they received and the personal commitment of their instructors.

———

Amber Glass Andrews is a graduate of Columbia Basin College in Pasco, Washington, and a pharmacist and lecturer at the University of Washington School of Pharmacy. "I attended CBC for two years to complete my pre-pharmacy course requirements. The science background I received there was exceptional and enabled me to enter the School of Pharmacy at the University of Washington."

———

What Community Colleges Cost. There are numerous advantages to enrolling in a community college instead of directly in a four-year college or university. One of them is the enormous savings that can be expected. A survey of the tuition charged by public two-year colleges during the fall of 1986 found the average tuition was $642. The lowest tuition was a mere $98, in California. The highest was $1,758, in Vermont. Only eight of fifty states charged $1,000 or more. In many states the tuition charged by public two-year colleges is between one-third and one-half the tuition charged by public four-year colleges and universities.

Many students can attend a community college for between $1,000 and $1,600 per year for tuition, books, and fees. An important factor is that this can be done while living at home, maintaining family ties and support, and even holding a job.

Comparing Costs. The following chart will help you understand how much money can be saved by attending a public community college before entering a four-year college. Tuition and fees are based on actual 1987 costs for a resident student attending college in the state of Ohio, which is representative of average national costs. Not taken into consideration are other charges—room and board, books and supplies, meals, transportation, telephone—that are nonexistent or cost substantially less at community colleges.

Options	1	2	3	4
Two years at a public community college	•		•	
Two years at a public four-year college	•			
Four years at a public four-year college		•		
Two years at a private four-year college			•	
Four years at a private four-year college				•
Total tuition and fees	**$6,606**	**$8,892**	**$16,430**	**$28,540**

Let's look at the comparison of these expenses for each of the options given. Suppose a student, John, wants to attend a state college or university. Because John is a resident of the state he will have to pay only the resident tuition and fees. Four years at the state college John selected will cost him $8,892. If on the other hand John decides to attend a nearby community college and then transfer to the state college for his last two years, his total bill for tuition and fees for both schools will be $6,606. If he takes the community college route, John will save $2,286 in tuition and fees alone.

John's high school classmate, Nancy, has her heart set on a private four-year university that's within commuting distance of her home. Nancy knows she will save her parents money by living at home, but what she doesn't know is how much more she could save them if she decided to attend the community college in the next town.

Nancy estimates the cost of tuition and fees at the four-year private university will be $28,540. If Nancy wants to save her parents even more money, she'll look into the costs at the community college. Two years there followed by two years at the private university will cost $16,430. That's over $12,000 in savings, and in the end Nancy will still have a degree from the prestigious private university.

Other Advantages. Attending a community college before enrolling in a four-year college or university is an excellent way to save money and still get a high-quality education. There are many other advantages to taking this route to a college degree. Let's look at some.

Working while going to college. Going to college in your own area gives you the possibility of working either full- or part-time to pay for your education. Because of the flexibility of class schedules at most community colleges you can mix day, night, and weekend classes. This permits you to set your classes around the requirements of your job.

Open admissions. Community colleges don't base their admissions on test scores or high school grades. They do require a high school diploma, but even if you don't have one, they conduct classes to prepare you for the high school equivalency test, the GED. Passing the GED qualifies you for admission. Many students who did poorly in high school and were unqualified for a four-year college have found that community college changed their attitude toward education. The majority of these "late bloomers" have gone on to earn a bachelor's degree. Community college gave them a second chance they might otherwise never have had.

Helping to find yourself. Several recent surveys found that a great many students entering college aren't sure about their future plans. If you fall into this category, community college offers you the opportunity to sample a wide variety of subject options, both educational and vocational. Should your goal be something more than a high school diploma, but you're not sure what, then a community college is an excellent place to sample what's available from higher education without having to commit yourself to a particular course of study.

If you're attending a two-year college and find that an academic education isn't right for you, it's easy to transfer to a vocational program. The same is true if you begin your college education in a vocational program and decide to change to an academic program with the option of continuing on to a four-year college.

Accessibility. Because community colleges are intended to serve the community in which they're built, it's usually easy for everyone to get to them. Most campuses are located within an urban center or are easily reached by public transportation.

The college environment. Both the student body and the faculty of most community colleges tend to be more representative of the larger community than do most four-year colleges. Because admissions policies aren't based on high school performance, test scores, and ability to pay or qualify for aid, the community college student body is more diversified.

Many students find the time they spend at a community college is not only educationally enriching but also broadens their horizons by presenting the opportunity to meet people they normally wouldn't have occasion to meet (entrepreneurs, professionals, housewives, people from other ethnic, racial, and social groups, etc.). This widening of personal contacts aids in the building of a much needed network for the future.

More than 50 percent of all college freshmen in the United States are enrolled in community colleges. Over one-third of the five million community college students are full-time. The average age for a student attending day classes is 23, while the average evening-classes student is 38 years old. Slightly less than one-quarter of the students are members of minorities, and nearly 50,000 are international students.

The faculty is usually more people-oriented with increased emphasis on teaching and less on grades. Faculty members are usually less academically oriented than in a university and tend to be more closely related to the "real world" their students must face when they go to work. This is most likely a product of the fact that over 60 percent of the over 230,000 community college faculty members teach part-time. Most work in the fields in which they teach, keeping them in closer touch with the changes and advances made in their fields.

Here's what some students have to say about the environment they found at their local community college:

> I attribute a lot of my success to the faculty and staff at LBC. They are the most caring group of people that I've ever had the pleasure to deal with.
>
> > Laura Mason
> > Linn-Benton Community College
> > Albany, OR

> This is really a very friendly place. The teachers here are great, they really care about their students. They're willing to take time with you, and their offices are always open.
>
> > Dave Vautrin
> > Orange Coast College
> > Costa Mesa, CA

Transferal of credits. Virtually every community and junior college in this country offers its students an academic program that enables them to transfer the credits earned to a four-year college or university. Most states have matriculation agreements that guarantee students who graduate from community colleges with associate's degrees acceptance at four-year state colleges. In addition, many community colleges work in cooperation with local private four-year colleges to ensure the academic classes they offer will satisfy the requirements of the private colleges for transfer acceptance. In other words, graduates of community colleges who earn transferable credits and are awarded an associate's degree will be able to transfer their community college credits to a four-year college or university where they will enter as juniors.

Here's what two graduates of Walla Walla Community College have to say about being able to transfer their credits to four-year colleges:

> Attending Walla Walla Community College was a very sound educational decision on my part. It not only saved me thousands of dollars, it prepared me for an easy transition into a four-year school (George Fox College, a private college in Newberg, OR). By receiving my A.A. degree, I was able to waive all my general requirements and step right into my upper division courses.

> Toby Long

> Walla Walla Community College was not only close and convenient, but also provided a good educational foundation with very little expense. This enabled me to go on to the University of Washington and enter dental school at Washington University in St. Louis.

> Doug Rietz

Financial aid. Community colleges offer a variety of financial aid programs similar to four-year colleges. These include federal and state programs, scholarships, loans, work study, and co-op programs.

Alternative means of earning credit. Many community colleges give credit for successfully passing proficiency examinations and for demonstrating knowledge gained through life experience. This offers students the opportunity to save even more money and time.

Attending a community college and then transferring your credits to a four-year college or university can be a smart move. Besides saving thousands of dollars, most students find community colleges to be a rewarding experience. Aside from the student who wants to save money, community colleges offer opportunities for those who have been burned-out by high school and need to make a gentle transition to college. It's ideal for the student with family problems who doesn't want to be away from home and needs the scheduling flexibility community colleges offer. It gives those who don't yet have educational goals the opportunity to experiment with different subjects and even take vocational courses along with academic ones.

The benefits of attending a community college are numerous and should be evaluated before you select a college. Visit the community college nearest you. You're sure to find people there who are more than willing to discuss your educational plans and how they might help.

5

A SCHOOL YEAR
IN YOUR MAILBOX

An increasingly popular method of reducing the cost of earning a college degree is to earn as many credits as possible through alternative education methods. This means you earn some of the credits required for your degree in ways other than attending traditional classes. In this and the following two chapters we'll examine three alternative education approaches to earning college credit that are available to most students. This includes full-time and part-time students.

The single most important factor in the use of alternative education is self-motivation. If you are motivated to spend the time and energy required to reduce the cost of your college education, the results may surprise you.

Study by Mail. One method that can save you both time and money is independent study through correspondence courses. Earning college credits through correspondence courses can help cut an entire year from the time you spend in college. In some colleges you can use correspondence courses to earn as much as half the credits required to be awarded a bachelor's degree. One reason these courses save you time is that they can be taken during the regular school year in addition to your scheduled classes. They can also be taken during summer vacations. Another benefit of these courses is that the per credit tuition charged for them is usually substantially less than the per credit charge for attending an equivalent class.

Correspondence study has come a long way since the days it was restricted to "home study" schools whose matchbook-cover advertisements promised well-paying careers if you took their courses.

Although once frowned on by many educators, credit-based correspondence courses are now offered by colleges and universities from coast to coast. Most are part of state university systems. These fully accredited educational institutions make available thousands of college courses that permit you to earn credits through the mail. The number of these correspondence courses increases each year.

Most of the colleges with comprehensive offerings of correspondence courses are members of the National University Extension Association. The association's primary goal is "to extend the resources of the university to meet the needs of an increasingly complex society."

For the truly motivated student who wants to make productive use of off-hours, correspondence courses can be an inexpensive and relatively painless way of earning credits. They permit you to work at a pace that should not interfere with your regular classroom responsibilities.

Get Permission. If you are a student in the college from which you plan to take correspondence courses, be sure to review this with the academic dean's office or similar authority to make sure the credits you earn will apply toward your degree requirements.

If the college you attend or want to attend doesn't offer correspondence based study, you must verify that it will accept transfer credits based on correspondence courses from another college. You should be able to get this information from the admissions office or the academic dean's office. It is best to bring along a copy of the catalogue descriptions of the correspondence courses you want to use for credit. This will enable the person from whom you are requesting permission to better understand the course, how it works, and how it may apply to your degree program. The explosive growth in nontraditional education makes it likely that most colleges will accept such credits, although there may be a limit on the number that can be transferred.

Later in this chapter, beginning on page 45, there is a directory of colleges and universities that offer a wide range and large number of correspondence courses for full credit. Each entry includes a brief description of the institution's policy concerning the maximum number of credits earned through correspondence courses that can be applied toward a bachelor's degree from that college or university.

The colleges and universities in this directory will be happy to send you a catalogue describing each correspondence course in depth. The catalogues explain the number of credits earned upon completion of the course, the cost, and additional information to help you select the correspondence courses most appropriate to your degree requirements. Carefully review the directory before writing or phoning those colleges with correspondence courses in the subjects you need.

Although most colleges refer to this method of learning as independent study, some continue calling it correspondence study or even home study. The trend is toward the term "independent study," recognizing the achievement of those students who complete these courses instead of where the work takes place, or the method used.

Is Independent Study for You? Before getting involved in any alternative education program, such as a correspondence course, first decide if this approach is right for you. Some people find drawbacks among what most consider the advantages of independent study. Your ability as a learner and your self-discipline are important factors for success. The rewards will not come without some sacrifice. Ask yourself if you are prepared to make the necessary sacrifices for these additional credits.

Completion of many credit-based correspondence courses requires more work on the student's part than participation in an equivalent classroom course. The advantage is that course work can be done at times and places appropriate to the student's schedule. While this is a clear advantage to the strongly motivated student, it can be a disaster to the one who is reluctant to commit off-hours to additional study. Before deciding on the use of correspondence courses to help reduce the cost and time of earning your degree, you must first ask yourself if you are willing to give up a portion of your social time. Studying for correspondence courses can't be done in place of studying for your traditional classes. It must be done in the time now spent on other activities; the sacrifice is, in most instances, your social life. If you are willing to forgo some social activities, then correspondence courses can help you earn your degree in less time and at less expense.

Don't rush off to mail in your correspondence course application just yet. There are several more questions you should answer first, including:

- Will I be able to maintain a study schedule in addition to my present school schedule?

- Can I do the work without the presence and regular assistance of an instructor?
- Can I learn college-level material outside the environment of a classroom?

The answer to these questions depends to a large extent on your motivation and ability to take control of your own time. It requires an honest evaluation of your capacity for learning. You alone must determine if you have the ability to commit yourself to independent study and be prepared to carry out that commitment.

William Armstrong, in his popular book *How to Study Effectively and Get Good Grades,* says the classroom contains an "atmosphere for achievement." He calls the student-teacher relationship a partnership. Establishing a similar relationship with your correspondence course instructor, while not impossible, is unlikely. Are you prepared to get along without this interaction? In most independent study programs it's not possible to conduct personal discussions with the instructors.

To sum up, correspondence courses offer the student who wants to save time earning a degree the opportunity to do so. In some colleges you can reduce the time by one full year through correspondence courses. If you decide independent study is something you're capable of doing, and you've considered the points we have discussed, enroll in a single course as a test. If you successfully complete it, you will be better able to assess the number of courses you can handle at any given time.

Who Can Enroll. Generally anyone with the desire and ability can enroll in a correspondence course from one of the colleges and universities in the directory in this chapter (pages 45–67). Transcripts and entrance examinations are not required, but be aware that a participant in a correspondence course is not automatically admitted as a resident student. College admission must be in line with the institution's admission policies.

It is your responsibility to select courses appropriate to your level of knowledge and educational goals. If a course requires a prerequisite course, you must be able to substantiate successful completion of the earlier course with a transcript.

Selecting a College. Once you've decided correspondence courses will play a role in your plan to reduce the cost of your college degree, you must decide what that role is and how large a part it will play. If you haven't yet selected the college you want to attend, review the list of colleges in the directory at the end of this chapter. To get the most benefit from correspondence courses, in terms of credits earned toward your degree, consider attending one of those colleges. The best combination for saving money is a college or university offering correspondence courses that is located close enough to your home to give you the cost-reduction benefit of commuting to classes, plus the time- and cost-saving benefits of correspondence courses.

If any of the colleges offering correspondence courses for credit are on the list of schools you would like to attend, send for both the general catalogue and correspondence catalogue. Consider the benefits of independent study as one of the criteria you use when making your final selection.

If none of the colleges in the directory are on your list, contact all the colleges you are considering and ask about their policy concerning the transfer of credits from another school when those credits are based on correspondence courses. If you plan on using correspondence courses to help cut your college costs, then each college's willingness to honor the credits you are awarded for successfully completing these courses must be one of the factors you use when making your final selection of a college to attend.

How Correspondence Courses Work. To help you decide if correspondence courses can be used to help cut your college costs, let's take a look at how they work.

Three to four weeks after mailing your course enrollment application you'll receive the course and all related materials. The textbook used for the course usually has to be ordered separately. You may be able to purchase it in your own college bookstore or, even better, at a nearby used-book store.

Included with the materials is a course syllabus, a study guide or set of supplemental instructions, and a series of assignments. When you finish a lesson, you mail the completed assignment to the college. An instructor, usually a faculty member, reviews your assignment and returns it with his or her comments and your grade.

The Final Examination. When all lessons for a course are completed, you take a proctored final examination. Some courses also require a proctored mid-term examination. If you're taking the correspondence course from the same college you're attending, the department offering the course provides facilities and a proctor for your final exam. The same is true if you live within commuting distance of the school.

A student who lives beyond commuting distance is required to locate someone to act as proctor who is acceptable to the college. The proctor could be a dean or department head at the student's resident college, or even a professor or student counselor. The rules for proctoring vary slightly from one college to another, but in any event it shouldn't be difficult to locate someone on campus who can meet the requirements to proctor your final exam.

After acceptance by the college your proctor receives the final examination for your course, which you must take in strict compliance with the rules. When the examination is completed, your proctor, who must be present while you take the exam, mails it back to the college for grading. If you can't take the final exam on the campus of the issuing college, any expenses incurred in obtaining the services of a proctor are paid by you.

Generally the score you receive on the final examination has a greater influence on your course grade than do the scores for the individual lessons, although maintaining acceptable grades throughout the course is important. The final exam for many correspondence courses is similar to that given students who have attended a comparable classroom-based course on the campus of the college offering the correspondence course.

Most correspondence courses cover the same material as a comparable classroom course, and require about the same amount of work. The courses are usually prepared by a member of the faculty, or are at least approved by faculty members who teach the specific courses.

Rules and Regulations. Although the rules for correspondence courses vary from one college to another, the following apply to most:

1. Most colleges offering correspondence courses limit the number of these courses you can take at one time to two, but some have no limit at all. If you are capable of taking more than two correspondence courses at once in addition to your regular classroom work, you can get around this rule by enrolling in correspondence courses from different colleges. Before you do so make sure of

two things: first, that you can successfully handle the increased work and second, that your resident college will accept the transfer of credits for *all* courses in which you're enrolling.

2. Students are generally given one year to complete the assignments and final exam for most correspondence courses. It's usually possible to obtain an extension, but there is normally an extra charge for this additional time. This extension policy is beneficial if you find you've taken on more work than you can handle to maintain satisfactory grades.

3. The rules for most correspondence courses limit the number of completed assignments that can be submitted at one time or the speed at which you can submit them. The reason for this is to allow you to review and benefit from the instructor's comments on previously submitted assignments before completing and mailing in new ones.

4. Enrollment in a correspondence course doesn't constitute enrollment at the college; however, some student privileges may be extended to correspondence students, such as use of the campus library.

Methods of Instruction. Correspondence courses make use of a variety of instruction methods that lend themselves to the overall experience of independent study. Some courses use traditional textbooks, while others use audiotapes or even videotapes as part of their instructional material.

If textbooks are used, they can be purchased from the college's bookstore if you like. Some colleges buy the books back from you when you've completed the course for about half the price you paid for them. When other instructional materials are used, such as audiotapes, the college will generally loan them to you. Inquire if there are any additional fees related to the use of audio or video materials.

Applying Your Credits. Earning credits through correspondence study offers you a unique opportunity to use your time productively in a program that provides enough flexibility so you can set your own pace and choose the time you want to study. Because of this, correspondence courses are more individualized than almost any other method of study.

When you have successfully completed all the lessons and the final examination, the college awards you the credits carried by the course. Most courses average three credits, but many carry anywhere from two to five credits. These credits can then be transferred to your department if you are a matriculating student at that college, or you can have a transcript sent to whatever college you wish.

The most important point to remember about taking a correspondence course is to obtain the permission of your academic dean or department head if you are going to take the course from the same school you are attending. If your college doesn't offer correspondence courses, be sure it will accept the transfer of these credits and that they are applicable toward your degree.

Colleges Offering Correspondence Courses for Credit. The charges quoted for correspondence courses from the following colleges were current at the time this book went to press. Be sure to contact the colleges whose courses you are interested in taking for any changes in price or availability.

ARIZONA STATE UNIVERSITY
University Continuing Education, Correspondence Study Office, Tempe, AZ 85287-1811; (602)965-6563

Arizona State students may apply a maximum of 30 semester-hours of correspondence course credit toward a baccalaureate. A three-credit course costs $99.

Correspondence courses are available in the following: business administration, communications, criminal justice, education, English, foreign languages, history, home economics, mathematics, physics, political science, psychology, sociology, speech and hearing sciences, and women's studies.

ARKANSAS STATE UNIVERSITY
Correspondence Division, Center for Continuing Education, P.O. Box 2260, State University, AR 72467-2260; (501)972-3052

A maximum of 31 hours of correspondence study may be applied toward a baccalaureate from Arkansas State. The fee for Arkansas residents for a three-credit course is $135. The fee for out-of-state students for a three-credit course is $159.

Correspondence courses are available in the following: accounting, administrative services, business administration, computer information systems, economics, English, geography, health, history, law enforcement, management, mathematics, political science, psychology, public relations, secondary education, sociology, social work, theater arts, and zoology.

AUBURN UNIVERSITY
Independent Study, 100 Mell Hall, Auburn University, AL 36849-5611; (205)826-5103

Students matriculating at Auburn can earn up to 25 percent of their required credits through correspondence courses. A three-credit course costs $72.

Correspondence courses are available in the following: economics, biology, building science, family and child development, geography, health education, history, nutrition and foods, physical education, political science, psychology, and vocational and adult education.

BALL STATE UNIVERSITY
School of Continuing Education, Director of Independent Study, 222 North College Avenue, Muncie, IN 47306; (317)285-5031

Up to 45 quarter-hours of independent study credits may be applied to a degree at Ball State. A three-credit course costs $111.

Correspondence courses are available in the following: accounting, astronomy, criminal justice, economics, English, geography, geology, history, journalism, philosophy, physics, political science, psychology, sociology, speech, and theater arts.

BRIGHAM YOUNG UNIVERSITY
Division of Continuing Education, Provo, UT 84602; (301)378-2868

Brigham Young undergraduates may apply up to 36 hours of independent study credits toward a bachelor's degree. A three-credit course costs $156.

Correspondence courses are available in the following: accounting, American heritage, animal science, anthropology, art history, art studio, biology, botany and range science, business management, career education, chemistry, civil engineering, clothing and textiles, communications, computer science, design engineering technology, economics, education, English, family sciences, food science and nutrition, French, genealogy, general studies, geography, geology, German, health sciences, Hebrew, history, humanities, industrial education, information management, Latin, library information sciences, managerial economics, mathematics, microbiology, nursing, organizational behavior, philosophy, physical education (dance), physical education (sports), physical science, physics and astronomy, political science, psychology, recreation management, religious education, social work, sociology, Spanish, statistics, theater–speech–cinema, youth leadership, and zoology.

CENTRAL MICHIGAN UNIVERSITY
School of Continuing Education and Community Services, Rowe 125, Mt. Pleasant, MI 48859; (517)774-3719

Students attending CMU may earn up to 15 credit-hours toward their degree through correspondence courses. A three-credit course costs $213.

Correspondence courses are available in the following: accounting, anthropology, art, biology, computer science, economics, education, educational administration, English, French, geography, German, health education, history, home economics, journalism, mathematics, physical education, physical science, physics, political science, psychology, recreation, sociology, Spanish, and speech.

COLORADO STATE UNIVERSITY
Division of Continuing Education, C102 Rockwell Hall, Fort Collins, CO 80523; (303)491-5288

The maximum number of credits earned through correspondence courses that can be applied toward a degree from Colorado State is set on an individual basis. The cost of a three-credit course is $120.

Correspondence courses are available in the following: adult education, agriculture, animal science, consumer sciences and housing, education, English, fishery and wildlife biology, food sciences and nutrition, history, human development and family studies, industrial sciences, outdoor recreation, and physical education.

EASTERN KENTUCKY UNIVERSITY
Division of Extended Programs, 27A Coates Building, Richmond, KY 40475-0931; (606)622-2003

Up to 32 semester-hours of credit may be earned through correspondence courses for a baccalaureate from Eastern Kentucky. A three-credit course costs $138.

Correspondence courses are available in the following: biological sciences, computer science, correctional services, criminal justice, economics, English, environmental science, geography, health education, history, management, marketing, mathematics, music, office administration, political science, psychology, real estate, science, security and loss prevention, social science, and sociology.

EASTERN MICHIGAN UNIVERSITY
Independent Study Office, Continuing Education, Ypsilanti, MI 48191; (313)487-1081

Up to 15 hours of correspondence course credit can be applied to an undergraduate degree. All courses carry three semester-hours of credit. The cost is $150 per course.

Correspondence courses are available in the following: business, English, history, mathematics, sociology, and technology.

INDIANA STATE UNIVERSITY
Independent Study Office, Continuing Education and Extended Services, Terre Haute, IN 47809; (812)232-6311, ext. 5567

A maximum of 30 semester-hours of credit may be applied toward a degree from Indiana State. A three-credit course costs $136.50.

Correspondence courses are available in the following: accounting, art history, astronomy, business education, criminology, education, educational psychology, English, French, geography, health and safety, history, journalism, Latin, life sciences, management–finance, mathematics, physical education, political science, psychology, social work, sociology, Spanish, and speech.

INDIANA UNIVERSITY
Independent Study Program, Owen Hall, Bloomington, IN 47405; (800)342-5410 in Indiana, (800)334-3693 out of state

Degree-seeking students should obtain approval for specific correspondence courses from the dean of the school or division from which they expect to graduate. A three-credit course costs $150.75.

Correspondence courses are available in the following: African studies, anthropology, apparel merchandising, astronomy, biology, business, classical studies, comparative literature, computer science, criminal justice, economics, education, English, fine arts, folklore, French, geography, geology, health, history, history and philosophy of science, interior design, Italian, journalism, labor studies, linguistics, mathematics, music, nursing, philosophy, physical education and recreation, physics, political science, psychology, public and environmental affairs, religious studies, sociology, Spanish, speech communications, and women's studies.

LOUISIANA STATE UNIVERSITY
Office of Independent Study, E 106 Pleasant Hall, Baton Rouge, LA 70803; (504)388-3171

Up to 25 percent of the total number of credit hours required for a bachelor's degree at LSU can be earned through correspondence courses. A three-credit course costs $110.

Correspondence courses are available in the following: accounting, agriculture, anthropology, astronomy, biology, business administration, communications, computer science, criminal justice, dairy science, economics, education, engineering graphics, English, environmental studies, finance, French, geography, geology, German, health education, history, home economics, industrial technology, interior design, Latin, management, marketing, mathematics, mechanical engineering, music, philosophy, physical science, psychology, quantitative business analysis, sociology, Spanish, speech communication, theater, vocational education, and zoology.

MISSISSIPPI STATE UNIVERSITY
Independent Study, P.O. Drawer 5247, Mississippi State, MS 39762; (601)325-3473

A maximum of 20 percent of any curriculum may be earned by independent study. A three-credit course costs $129.

Correspondence courses are available in the following: accounting, business education, business statistics, computer science, counselor education, economics, educational psychology, elementary education, engineering graphics, finance, foreign languages, home economics, history, marketing, mathematics, microbiology, philosophy and religion, physical education, physics, political science, psychology, social work, sociology, special education, and wildlife.

MURRAY STATE UNIVERSITY
Extended Education, Sparks Hall, Murray, KY 42071; (502)762-3011

Murray State students may apply to their degree program a maximum of 32 credits earned through correspondence courses. A three-credit course costs $90.

Correspondence courses are available in the following: accounting, agriculture, animal science, English, health education, history, legal studies, mathematics, office administration, political science, psychology, recreation and physical education, and sociology.

OHIO UNIVERSITY
Independent Study, 302 Tupper Hall, Athens, OH 45701-2979; (800)282-4408 in Ohio, (800)342-4791 out of state

There is no limit on the number of independent study credits which can be applied toward an Ohio University degree. A three-credit course costs $120.

Correspondence courses are available in the following: accounting, art history, aviation, botany, business administration, business law, business management and technology, chemistry, economics, education, elementary education, English, English literature, finance, foreign languages, geography, government, health, history, home economics, humanities, human resource management, interpersonal communications, journalism, law enforcement technology, library media technology, marketing, mathematics, music, philosophy, and physical education.

OKLAHOMA STATE UNIVERSITY
Independent and Correspondence Study Department, 001 Classroom Building, Stillwater, OK 74078-0404; (405)624-6340

Up to 25 percent of the hours required for a degree at Oklahoma State may be taken through correspondence courses. A three-credit course costs $105.

Correspondence courses are available in the following: accounting, agricultural education, agronomy, animal science, anthropology, applied behavioral studies in education, astronomy, biological sciences, business administration, business law, chemistry, computing and information science, curriculum and instruction education, economics, electronics engineering technology, engineering science, English, family relations and child development, fire protection and safety technology, food and nutrition, French, general administration, general technology, geography, geology, German, health, history, horticulture, housing interior design, industrial engineering, interdisciplinary studies, journalism and broadcasting, library science, management, marketing, mathematics, music, petroleum technology, philosophy, physics, political science, psychology, sociology, Spanish, speech pathology, statistics, theater, trade and industrial education, and university studies.

PENNSYLVANIA STATE UNIVERSITY
Department of Independent Learning, 128 Mitchell Building, University Park, PA 16802; (800)252-3592 in Pennsylvania, (800)458-3617 out of state

There is no maximum number of correspondence course credits that can be applied toward a bachelor's degree from Penn State. A three-credit course costs $180.

Correspondence courses are available in the following: accounting, American studies, anthropology, art history, biology, business law, business logistics, civil engineering, classics, comparative literature, computer science, economics, educational psychology, electrical engineering, engineering, engineering graphics, engineering mechanics, English, finance, food service and housing administration, French, German, history, hotel and food service, individual and family studies, industrial education, industrial engineering, journalism, labor studies, law enforcement and corrections, mathematics, mechanical engineering, meteorology, music, nursing, nutrition, philosophy, physical education, physics, political science, psychology, quantitative business analysis, religious studies, Russian, social science, Spanish, statistics, and theater.

PORTLAND STATE UNIVERSITY
Independent Study, P.O. Box 1491, Portland OR 97207; (800)452-4909, ext. 4865, in Oregon, (800)547-8887, ext. 4865, out of state

The number of correspondence course credits that can be applied toward a Portland State degree is determined by the appropriate deans. The cost of a three-credit course can range from $40 to $123.

Correspondence courses are available in the following: administration of justice, animal science, anthropology, architecture, art, atmospheric science, business administration, citizenship, computer science, economics, education, engineering, English, foreign languages, geography, geology, health, history, mathematics, physical science, psychology, religion, and secretarial science.

ROOSEVELT UNIVERSITY
College of Continuing Education, 430 South Michigan Avenue, Chicago, IL 60605; (312)341-3866

There is no limit to the number of correspondence course credits that can be applied toward a Roosevelt University degree. The cost of a three-credit course is $194.

Correspondence courses are available in the following: accounting, economics, geography, geology, literature, mathematics, physical science, and political science.

TEXAS TECH UNIVERSITY
Independent Study by Correspondence, Division of Continuing Education, P.O. Box 4110, Lubbock, TX 79409-2191; (806)742-2352

A maximum of 18 credits earned through correspondence courses may be applied toward a degree at Texas Tech. A three-credit course costs $114.

Correspondence courses are available in the following: accounting, agricultural economics, agricultural science, animal science, anthropology, biblical literature, business law, economics, education, English, family studies, finance, food and nutrition, geography, geoscience, government, health, history, human development, information systems and quantitative sciences, management, mathematics, marketing, mass communications, music, philosophy, physical education and recreation, plant and soil science, political science, psychology, religion, and sociology.

UNIVERSITY OF ALABAMA
College of Independent Studies, P.O. Box 2967, Tuscaloosa, AL 35486-2967; (205)348-7626, (800)452-5971 in Alabama only

Twenty-five percent of the credits required for a bachelor's degree may be earned through correspondence courses. The cost of a three-credit course is $135.

Correspondence courses are available in the following: accounting, American studies, anthropology, astronomy, biology, business administration, chemical engineering, classics, consumer sciences, counselor education, criminal justice, economics, English, finance, general studies, geography, German, health-care management, health education, history, human development and family life, human resources management, Latin, legal studies, marketing, mass communications, mathematics, music academics, nutrition, philosophy, physical education, physics, political science, Portuguese, psychology, religious studies, social work, sociology, Spanish, statistics, and theater history.

UNIVERSITY OF ALASKA
Correspondence Study, 115 Eielson Building, Fairbanks, AK 99775-0560; (907)474-7222

The University of Alaska will accept 32 credit-hours of correspondence study toward a bachelor's degree, and 15 credit-hours of correspondence study toward an associate degree. A three-credit course costs $90.

Correspondence courses are available in the following: accounting, Alaska native studies, anthropology, applied statistics, aviation technology, biology, business administration, chemistry, computer information systems, economics, education, English, Eskimo, geography, geoscience, health sciences, history, humanities, journalism and broadcasting, justice, library science, linguistics, mathematics, music, office occupations, political science, petroleum technology, psychology, sociology, and speech communication.

UNIVERSITY OF ARIZONA
Continuing Education, Independent Study Through Correspondence, 1717 East Speedway, Room 3205, Tucson, AZ 85719; (602)621-1896

A maximum of 60 semester-hours of independent study may be applied toward an undergraduate degree at the University of Arizona. A three-credit course costs $174.

Correspondence courses are available in the following: accounting, American Indian studies, animal sciences, anthropology, atmospheric sciences, black studies, business and career education, economics, educational foundations, educational psychology, English, entomology, finance, French, general biology, geosciences, German, health education, history, home economics, management, marketing, mathematics, oriental studies, philosophy, plant pathology, political science, renewable natural resources, sociology, and Spanish.

UNIVERSITY OF ARKANSAS
Department of Independent Study, 346 West Avenue, Fayetteville, AR 72701; (501)575-3647, (800)632-0035 in Arkansas only

A University of Arkansas student may apply a maximum of 30 correspondence course credits toward an undergraduate degree. A three-credit course costs $90.

Correspondence courses are available in the following: agricultural economics, animal sciences, anthropology, Bible, botany, business administration, education, engineering, engineering science, English, French, geography, German, health education, history, home economics, industrial engineering, mathematics, philosophy, physical education, political science, psychology, recreation, secondary education, social welfare, sociology, Spanish, speech, vocational teacher education, Western civilization, world literature, and zoology.

UNIVERSITY OF CALIFORNIA–EXTENSION
Lifelong Learning, 2223 Fulton Street, Berkeley, CA 94720; (415)642-4124

The acceptance of credit earned through independent study toward degree requirements is under the jurisdiction of the colleges and universities that grant the degrees. The fee for a three-credit course is generally $220.

Correspondence courses are available in the following: anthropology, art, astronomy, biochemistry, biological sciences, business and management, career planning and personal development, chemistry, computer science, economics, education, engineering, English, geology, history, horticulture, languages, labor relations law, mathematics, music, nutritional sciences, pest management, philosophy, physics, political science, psychology, public health, radiologic technology, real estate, sociology, statistics, and writing.

UNIVERSITY OF COLORADO
Division of Continuing Education, Campus Box 178, Boulder, CO 80309; (303)492-8756

The maximum number of credits earned through correspondence courses that can be applied to a degree from the University of Colorado is set on an individual basis. The cost of a three-credit course is $126.

Correspondence courses are available in the following: anthropology, business accounting, economics, education, engineering, English, fine arts, geography, geology, history, mathematics, music, philosophy, physical education, political science, psychology, and sociology.

UNIVERSITY OF FLORIDA
Independent Study by Correspondence, 1223 NW 22nd Avenue, Gainesville, FL 32609; (904)392-1711

Students attending the University of Florida must obtain the approval of a college official to receive credit toward their degree through independent study. Costs vary. A three-credit course is approximately $85.

Correspondence courses are available in the following: agriculture, anthropology, art, astronomy, business administration, chemistry, criminal justice, economics, education, English, geography, geology, German, health education, history, home economics, humanities, insurance, journalism and communications, liberal studies, management, marketing, mathematics, philosophy, political science, psychology, religion, sociology, special education, and statistics.

UNIVERSITY OF GEORGIA
Georgia Center for Continuing Education, Athens, GA 30602; (404)542-3243

Correspondence courses may be used to complete up to 25 percent of the hours required to earn a bachelor's degree from the University of Georgia. A three-credit course costs $120.

Correspondence courses are available in the following: accounting, agriculture, anthropology, art history, banking and finance, biology, business administration, classical culture, criminal justice, economics, education, English, entomology, environmental sciences, French, geography, German, health education, history, home economics, journalism and mass communication, Latin, legal studies, management, management sciences and information technology, marketing, mathematics, philosophy, political science, psychology, public administration, religion, sociology, Spanish, speech communication, and veterinary medicine.

UNIVERSITY OF IDAHO
Correspondence Study in Idaho, CEB 16, Moscow, ID 83843; (208)885-6641

This program is administered for all four state colleges in Idaho. A maximum of 32 nonresident credits (including correspondence courses) can be applied toward earning a bachelor's degree from Idaho State University, Lewis-Clark State College, and Boise State University. At the University of Idaho the maximum is 48 nonresident credits. The fee for a three-credit course is $135.75.

Correspondence courses are available in the following: accounting, agricultural economics, agricultural education, anthropology, bacteriology, biology, business and marketing, business education, consumer economics, criminal justice, economics, education, electrical engineering, engineering graphics, engineering science, English, foreign languages, forestry–wildlife and range sciences, history, home economics, library science, mathematics, philosophy, physics, political science, psychology, real estate, sociology, special education, and vocational education.

UNIVERSITY OF ILLINOIS
Guided Individual Study, Suite 1406, 302 East John Street, Champaign, IL 61820; (217)333-1321

Up to 60 hours of correspondence instruction may be applied toward a bachelor's degree from the University of Illinois. The cost of a three-credit course is $132.

Correspondence courses are available in the following: anthropology, business, education, engineering science, geography, history, languages, mathematics, physics, political science, psychology, rhetoric, sociology, theoretical and applied mechanics, urban planning, and vocational and technical education.

UNIVERSITY OF IOWA
Division of Continuing Education, W. 400 Sea Shore Hall, Iowa City, IA 52242; (319)353-4963, (800)272-6430 in Iowa only

A maximum of 30 semester-hours of credit earned through correspondence study may be applied toward an undergraduate degree at the University of Iowa. A three-credit course costs $105.

Correspondence courses are available in the following: accounting, American studies, anthropology, business administration, chemistry, communications, drawing, economics, education, educational counseling, educational psychology, elementary education, engineering, English, French, geography, Greek, history, home economics, journalism, literature, marketing, mathematics, music, nutrition, physical education, police science, political science, psychology, religion, social work, sociology, Spanish, speech and dramatic art, and statistics.

UNIVERSITY OF KANSAS
Continuing Education Building, Independent Study, Lawrence, KS 66045-2606; (913)864-4440

The maximum credits earned through correspondence courses applicable to a University of Kansas bachelor's degree are set by each department. The cost of a three-credit course is $129.

Correspondence courses are available in the following: African studies, anthropology, art history, biology, business, classics, communication studies, economics, education, engineering, English, French, geography, German, health, history, human development and family life, journalism and mass communications, Latin, mathematics, meteorology, philosophy, physical education and recreation, political science, psychology, religious studies, sociology, and Spanish.

UNIVERSITY OF KENTUCKY
University Extension, Independent Study Program, 1 Frazee Hall, Lexington, KY 40506-0031; (800)432-0963 in Kentucky, (800)325-2766 out of state, (606)257-3466

The maximum number of correspondence course credits that can be applied toward an undergraduate degree at the University of Kentucky varies by department. Contact the appropriate academic dean for further information. A three-credit course costs $168.

Correspondence courses are available in the following: accounting, agriculture, agronomy, animal sciences, biology, business and office technology, classical languages and literature, community health, economics, education and counseling psychology, engineering, English, family studies, finance, forestry, French language and literature, geography, German language and literature, history, home economics, human environment, journalism, management, marketing, mathematics, music, nutrition and food science, philosophy, physics and astronomy, political science, psychology, social work, sociology, Spanish language and literature, and statistics.

UNIVERSITY OF MICHIGAN
Extension Service, Department of Independent Study, 412 Maynard Street, Ann Arbor, MI 48109; (313)764-5311

The University of Michigan accepts 15 hours of credit earned through correspondence courses as applicable toward an undergraduate degree. The cost of a three-credit course is $330.

Correspondence courses are available in the following: accounting, American culture, Asian studies, economics, education, English, French, geography, German, great books, history, mathematics, natural resources, psychology, and science.

UNIVERSITY OF MINNESOTA
Extension Independent Study, 45 Westbrook Hall, 77 Pleasant Street SE, Minneapolis, MN 55455; (612)625-3333

A maximum of 50 percent of the credits required for a bachelor of arts degree at the University of Minnesota may be earned through independent study. A three-credit course costs $125.25.

Correspondence courses are available in the following: accounting, aerospace engineering, Afro-American studies, agricultural economics, American studies, animal science, anthropology, architecture, art, Asian studies, astronomy, biology, business law, business studies, child psychology, chemistry, civil engineering, classics, computer sciences, criminal justice, data processing, design, East Asian studies, ecology, economics, education, electrical engineering, English, entomology, family studies, finance, food science and nutrition, forestry, French, geography, geology and geophysics, German, Greek, health sciences, history, horticultural science, humanities, industrial engineering, industrial relations, insurance, Italian, Jewish studies, journalism and mass communications, Latin, law, linguistics, management, marketing, mathematics, mechanical engineering, music, Norwegian, operations management, pharmacy, philosophy, physics, Polish, political science, Portuguese, psychology, public affairs, public health, religious studies, rhetoric, Russian, Scandinavian, social studies, social work, sociology, Spanish, statistics, study skills, Swedish, textiles, theater arts, veterinary medicine, and women's studies.

UNIVERSITY OF MISSISSIPPI
Division of Continuing Education, University, MS 38677; (601)232-7282

Students who expect to earn an undergraduate degree from the University of Mississippi must consult their dean regarding the maximum number of credits they can earn through correspondence courses. A three-credit course costs $120.

Correspondence courses are available in the following: accounting, art, astronomy, biology, business education, chemistry, computer science, economics, education, English, finance, French, German, health education, history, home economics, interdisciplinary science, journalism, Latin, library science, management, marketing, mathematics, music, office administration, philosophy, physics, political science, psychology, religion, Russian, sociology, Spanish, and speech.

UNIVERSITY OF MISSOURI
Center for Independent Study, 136 Clark Hall, Columbia, MO 65211; (314)882-2491

Up to 30 semester-hours of credit earned through independent study may be applied toward a bachelor's degree from the University of Missouri. A three-credit course costs approximately $150.

Correspondence courses are available in the following: accounting, agriculture, anthropology, atmospheric science, chemistry, classical studies, economics, education, engineering, English, entomology, finance, geology, geography, history, health service management, home economics, horticulture, hospital administration, journalism, management, marketing, mathematics, peace studies, philosophy, physical education, political science, psychology, recreation and park administration, religion, romance languages, social work, special education, statistics, and women's studies.

UNIVERSITY OF NEBRASKA–LINCOLN
College Independent Study, Division of Continuing Studies, 33rd and Holdrege Streets, Lincoln, NB 68583; (402)472-1926

The colleges of the University of Nebraska allow from 25 to 60 semester-hours of independent study to be applied toward a bachelor's degree. The cost of a three-credit course is $150.

Correspondence courses are available in the following: accountancy, art, biological sciences, broadcasting, classics, curriculum and instruction, economics, educational psychology, English, finance, food service management, geography, health and physical education, history, human development and the family, human nutrition, industrial and management systems engineering, journalism, management, marketing, mathematics and statistics, philosophy, physics and astronomy, political science, psychology, real estate, and sociology.

UNIVERSITY OF NEVADA–RENO
Independent Study and Continuing Education, Reno, NV 89557-0081; (702)784-4652

Students in the University of Nevada system may earn a maximum of 60 credits through correspondence study to apply toward a bachelor's degree. A three-credit course costs $108.

Correspondence courses are available in the following: accounting, anthropology, biology, computer sciences, curriculum and instruction, economics, education, English, French, geography, German, history, home economics, hotel administration, Italian, journalism, mathematics, nursing, political science, psychology, sociology, and Spanish.

UNIVERSITY OF NEW MEXICO
Division of Continuing Education, 1634 University Boulevard N.E., Albuquerque, NM 87131; (505)277-2931

A maximum of 30 credits earned through independent study may be applied toward an undergraduate degree. The cost of a three-credit course is $135.

Correspondence courses are available in the following: anthropology, business education, chemistry, curriculum and instruction, economics, education, educational media and library science, English, geology, history, management, mathematics and statistics, nursing, philosophy, physics and astronomy, political science, psychology, sociology, and Spanish.

UNIVERSITY OF NORTH CAROLINA–CHAPEL HILL
Independent Study by Correspondence, 121 Abernathy Hall 002 A, Chapel Hill, NC 27514; (919)962-1106

This program is administered for a consortium of colleges and universities. The maximum number of correspondence course credits that can be applied toward a bachelor's degree for each of these institutions is: Appalachian State University, 20; Elizabeth City State University, 24; North Carolina State University, limit set by each department; University of North Carolina–Asheville, 30; University of North Carolina–Chapel Hill, 30; University of North Carolina–Greensboro, no limit; Western Carolina University, set by each department; Winston-Salem State University, 30. A three-credit course costs $120.

Correspondence courses are available in the following: accounting, anthropology, business, chemistry, classics, coastal marine studies, computer science, dramatic art, economics, education, electrical engineering, English, environmental sciences, French, geography, geology, German, health administration, history, home economics, interdisciplinary studies, Italian, Latin, mathematics, music, philosophy, physics, political science, poultry science, psychology, recreational administration, religion, Russian, sociology, Spanish, statistics, and university studies.

UNIVERSITY OF NORTH DAKOTA
Department of Correspondence Study, Box 8277, University Station, Grand Forks, ND 58202; (701)777-3044, (800)342-8230 in North Dakota only

A maximum of 30 hours of credit toward a degree from the University of North Dakota can be earned through correspondence study. A three-credit course costs $120.

Correspondence courses are available in the following: accounting, business and vocational education, computer science, education, engineering, English language and literature, French, geography, German, history, home economics, humanities, Latin, management, marketing, mathematics, Norwegian, pharmacology, political science, psychology, religion, sociology, Spanish, and visual arts.

UNIVERSITY OF NORTHERN COLORADO
Continuing Education Services, Greeley, CO 80639; (303)351-2944

The maximum number of credits earned through correspondence courses that can be applied toward a degree from the University of Northern Colorado is set on an individual basis. The cost of all courses is based on $32 per credit.

Correspondence courses are available in the following: biology, economics, education, fishery and wildlife biology, geography, home economics, humanities, mathematics, political science, and vocational education.

UNIVERSITY OF NORTHERN IOWA
Correspondence Study, 144 Gilchrist Hall, Cedar Falls, IA 50614; (319)273-2123, (800)772-1746 in Iowa only

A maximum of 25 percent of the work required for either an Iowa teaching certificate or a bachelor of arts degree from the University of Northern Iowa may be earned through correspondence courses. The cost of a three-credit course is $141.

Correspondence courses are available in the following: accounting, business education, earth science, economics, elementary education, educational psychology, English, geography, health, history, home economics, humanities, management, mathematics, modern languages, political science, religion, social work, and sociology.

UNIVERSITY OF OKLAHOMA
Independent Study Department, 1700 Asp Avenue, Room B-1, Norman, OK 73037; (405)325-1921, (800)942-5702 in Oklahoma only

Up to 30 credits earned through correspondence courses may be applied to a University of Oklahoma undergraduate degree. A three-credit course costs $105.

Correspondence courses are available in the following: accounting, anthropology, art, astronomy, business communication, business law, chemistry, classics, communication, drama, economics, education, engineering, English, French, geography, German, government, Greek, history, home economics, Italian, Japanese, journalism, Latin, law enforcement technology, library science, marketing, mathematics, mechanics, modern literature, music, personal finance, philosophy, physical education, political science, professional writing, psychology, social work, sociology, and zoology.

UNIVERSITY OF SOUTH CAROLINA
Department of Independent Study, Division of Continuing Education, Columbia, SC 29208; (803)777-2188

A total of 30 semester-hours of credit earned through correspondence study may be applied toward a degree from the University of South Carolina. The cost of a three-credit course is $90.

Correspondence courses are available in the following: accounting, business administration, criminal justice, economics, education, English, French, general studies, geography, German, government and international studies, health, history, Latin, management, marketing, mathematics, philosophy, physical education, physics, psychology, sociology, and Spanish.

UNIVERSITY OF SOUTH DAKOTA
State-Wide Educational Services, Center for Continuing Education, Vermillion, SD 57069; (605)677-5281, (800)952-3670 in South Dakota only

A maximum of 30 credits earned through correspondence courses may be applied toward a University of South Dakota bachelor's degree in the College of Arts & Sciences, the College of Fine Arts, and the School of Education. A three-credit course costs $144.

Correspondence courses are available in the following: alcohol- and drug-abuse studies, anthropology, art, astronomy, business, classics, communication disorders, criminal justice, earth sciences, education, English, geography, history, mathematics, modern languages, political science, psychology, and social behavior.

UNIVERSITY OF SOUTHERN MISSISSIPPI
Office of Independent Study, Southern Station, Box 5056, Hattiesburg, MS 39406-5056; (601)266-4206

Up to 25 percent of the requirements for a bachelor's degree at the University of Southern Mississippi may be earned through independent study. A three-credit course costs $129.

Correspondence courses are available in the following: accounting, biology, business education, coaching and sports administration, computer science, economics, engineering technology, English, finance, foreign languages, general business administration, geography, geology, health, history, hotel and restaurant administration, industrial and vocational education, journalism, management, marketing, mathematics, philosophy and religion, physical education, political science, psychology, real estate and insurance, recreation, research and foundations, science education, sociology and anthropology, and therapy.

UNIVERSITY OF TENNESSEE
Center for Extended Learning, 420 Communications and Extension Building, Knoxville, TN 37996; (615)974-5134

Twenty-five percent of the total undergraduate credit for a University of Tennessee degree may be earned through independent study. This applies to all of the campuses—Knoxville, Chattanooga, and Martin. A three-credit course costs $102.

Correspondence courses are available in the following: accounting, agricultural economics, anthropology, astronomy, broadcasting, business management, chemistry, child and family studies, criminal justice, economics, electrical engineering, education, English, forestry, French, geography, geology, German, health and safety, history, industrial engineering, Italian, journalism, mathematics, nutrition, philosophy, political science, psychology, religious studies, sociology, Spanish, and zoology.

UNIVERSITY OF TEXAS–AUSTIN
Independent Learning EIMC, P.O. Box 7700, Austin, TX 78713-7700; (512)471-7716 or -5616

A maximum of 30 percent of the credits required for a bachelor's degree from the University of Texas may be earned through independent study. The cost of a three-credit course is $108.

Correspondence courses are available in the following: anthropology, art, astronomy, biological sciences, business communications, business law, classics, curriculum and instruction, Czech, economics, educational psychology, English, French, geography, German, government, Greek, history, home economics, international business, Italian, management, marketing, mathematics, Middle Eastern studies, nursing, pharmacy, philosophy, physical and health education, physics, Portuguese, psychology, sociology, Spanish, and special education.

UNIVERSITY OF UTAH

Correspondence Study, Division of Continuing Education, 308 Park Building, Salt Lake City, UT 84112; (801)581-6473

A maximum of 25 percent of the credits required for a degree from the University of Utah may be earned through correspondence study. A three-credit course costs $90.

Correspondence courses are available in the following: accounting, anthropology, art, biology, civil engineering, communications, economics, educational administration, educational studies, education, English, family and consumer studies, finance, foods and nutrition, geography, health education, history, languages, journalism, library science, management, marketing, mathematics, metallurgy, meteorology, music, physical education, physics, political science, psychology, recreation and leisure, secretarial training, sociology, special education, and writing.

UNIVERSITY OF WASHINGTON

Distance Learning, 5001 25th Avenue NE, GH-23, Seattle, WA 98195; (206)543-2350

A maximum of 50 percent of the credits required for an undergraduate degree from the University of Washington may be earned through independent study. A three-credit course costs $105.

Correspondence courses are available in the following: American Indian studies, anthropology, astronomy, atmospheric sciences, braille, business, chemistry, economics, education, engineering, English, foreign languages, geography, gerontology, history, linguistics, mathematics, music, nursing, oceanography, philosophy, physical therapy, political science, psychology, rehabilitation medicine, religious studies, sociology, statistics, urban planning, wildland recreation, and women's studies.

UNIVERSITY OF WISCONSIN

227 Extension Building, 432 North Lake Street, Madison, WI 53706; (608)262-2011, (608)263-2055

The last 32 credits toward an undergraduate degree must be earned on campus. Other than that there is no specified limit on the number of correspondence course credits that may be applied toward a degree. A three-credit course costs $126.

Correspondence courses are available in the following: agriculture, anthropology, Arabic, art, botany, business, chemistry, classics, comparative literature, computer sciences, Danish, disaster management, economics, education, educational psychology, engineering, English, forestry, French, geography, geology, German, Greek, Hebrew and Semitic studies, history, horse science, Italian, journalism and mass communication, Latin, linguistics, literature in translation, mathematics, meteorology, music, Norwegian, nursing, philosophy, physics, Polish, political science, Portuguese, psychology, recreation resources, Russian, social work, sociology, Spanish, statistics, Swedish, and women's studies.

UNIVERSITY OF WYOMING
Correspondence Study Department, Box 3294 University Station, Laramie, WY 82071; (307)766-6323

As many as 24 semester-hours toward a bachelor's degree at the University of Wyoming may be earned by the completion of correspondence study courses. A three-credit course costs $99.

Correspondence courses are available in the following: accounting, administration, adult education, agricultural economics, animal sciences, anthropology, art, astronomy, business administration, business education, civil engineering, communication, computer science, curriculum and instruction, economics, engineering science, English, entomology, food sciences, foundations and instructional technology, geography, health education, history, home economics, journalism and telecommunication, languages, mathematics, molecular biology, music, physical education, political science, psychology, statistics, sociology, and theater and dance.

UTAH STATE UNIVERSITY
Independent Study Division, Life Span Learning Programs, Logan, UT 84322-5000; (801)750-2028

A total of 45 independent study credits may be used toward fulfilling the requirements for a bachelor's degree from Utah State. The cost of a three-credit course is $75.

Correspondence courses are available in the following: accounting, administrative systems, agricultural economics, animal science, anthropology, art, biometeorology, biology, business administration, business education, civil and environmental engineering, communicative disorders, dairy science, economics, elementary education, engineering, English, entomology, family and human development, fisheries and wildlife, forest resources, geography, geology, health education, history, industrial technology and education, instructional technology, landscape architecture and environmental planning, languages, mathematics, microbiology, music, nutrition and food sciences, occupational safety and health, philosophy, physical education and recreation, physiology, plant science, psychology, public health, range science, secondary education, social work, sociology, soil science, special education, and veterinary science.

WASHINGTON STATE UNIVERSITY
Van Doren Hall Room 7, Continuing University Studies, Courses by Correspondence, Pullman, WA 99163; (509)335-2339, (800)556-0556 in Washington only

Washington State students may complete a maximum of 25 percent of the total number of hours required for a bachelor's degree through correspondence study. A three-credit course costs $126.

Correspondence courses are available in the following: agronomy, architecture, business administration, criminal justice, economics, engineering, English, entomology, food and nutrition, German, history, horticulture, humanities, philosophy, political science, psychology, sociology, Spanish, and speech.

WESTERN KENTUCKY UNIVERSITY
Office of Independent Study, 203 Van Meter Hall, Bowling Green, KY 42101; (502)745-4158

A maximum of 25 percent of the credits required for a degree from Western Kentucky University may be earned by correspondence. The cost of a three-credit course is $135.

Correspondence courses are available in the following: accounting, administrative office systems, anthropology, biology, communication and theater, economics, English, geography, government, health and safety, history, mathematics, physical education and recreation, psychology, and sociology.

WESTERN MICHIGAN UNIVERSITY
Division of Continuing Education, Office of Self-Instructional Programs, Kalamazoo, MI 49008; (616)383-0788

A maximum of 30 credits from correspondence courses may be applied toward an undergraduate degree from Western Michigan. A three-credit course costs $205.

Correspondence courses are available in the following: American studies, anthropology, biology, business information systems, chemistry, computer science, consumer resources and technology, counselor education and counseling psychology, economics, education, engineering technology, English, general humanities, general studies, geography, health and human services, industrial engineering, mathematics, medical studies, medieval studies, occupational therapy, philosophy, political science, psychology, sociology, and vocational education.

WESTERN WASHINGTON UNIVERSITY
Independent Study Office, University Extension, Bellingham, WA 98225; (206)676-3650

A maximum of 45 credits by correspondence courses may be applied to a bachelor's degree from Western Washington. A three-credit course costs $105.

Correspondence courses are available in the following: accounting, American cultural studies, anthropology, East Asian studies, education, English, history, home economics, mathematics, psychology, sociology, and technology.

6

EARNING CREDIT FOR WHAT YOU ALREADY KNOW

Few of us go through the daily experiences of our lives without learning something. A question we should ask ourselves is, "Is what I have learned of real value?" In this chapter we'll discuss how you can answer that question. We will also discuss how you can determine if that learning is of such value that it can help you cut your college costs by translating it into college credits that can be applied toward your degree.

Experiential Learning. A rewarding way of earning college credits outside the classroom is a process that evaluates knowledge you already possess. Knowledge can be acquired through a job you've held, a hobby, travel, personal reading, noncredit courses you've taken, volunteer work, or any other activity through or from which you have learned something. Learning gained through one's life experiences is called *experiential learning.* The evaluation of experiential learning is the testing or documentation of your knowledge and competency or skills. As you read through this chapter it's important to keep in mind that college credits are awarded not for experience but for knowledge and skills.

Special Assessment. The process used to evaluate your experiential learning to determine if it is worth college credits is called a *special assessment.*

The goal of a special assessment is to establish if the knowledge you've gained from informal learning experiences is equivalent to that you would receive if you took a college course on the same subject. If the determination is favorable, you will usually be awarded the same number of college credits you would had you taken and passed the course.

An important point to keep in mind is that a special assessment evaluates not your life experiences but what you've learned from those experiences. Special assessments are generally conducted to evaluate knowledge in a particular subject, although it is possible to appraise an entire body of knowledge, covering several subject areas.

Most colleges have a special assessment program that awards credits for demonstrating experiential learning. The number of credits you can earn through special assessments depends on the policies of the individual schools. Many colleges allow 25 percent or more of the credits required for a degree to be earned through special assessments. This can save you one entire year in earning your degree and the expenses associated with it, such as tuition, room, and board.

If the college you are attending doesn't have a special assessment program, ask if you can transfer credits received through a special assessment conducted at another college. This information can usually be obtained from the academic dean's office. If the answer is yes, review the information contained in the Appendix, *College Profiles for Cost Cutters.* Locate a college nearby that awards credit for what you've learned through your life experiences. It may be possible to have the special assessment done at that college and the credits transferred to the college you are attending. The appendix contains the names of over one thousand colleges and universities that have active programs for evaluating experiential learning.

If you have not yet selected a college, and you believe that an assessment of the knowledge you've gained through your life experiences will result in your being awarded a substantial amount of college credits, then you should seriously consider as candidates colleges and universities that award credit for experiental learning.

To help you determine which colleges are potential candidates for selection, the last section of this chapter (beginning on page 75) contains information on the policies of many colleges and universities regarding the maximum number of college credits they will award through a special assessment of experiential learning. This more complete information is available for only a small number of the institutions included in the appendix because many colleges don't have a firm policy on this matter. In these colleges each student's case is treated individually, based on his or her knowledge and competency.

How Special Assessment Works. Although policies vary from one college to another, special assessments are usually made for subjects that can't be evaluated in another way, such as the proficiency examinations discussed in Chapter 7.

There are three basic formats used in special assessments that evaluate your experiential learning. Most evaluations will take one of the following forms:

- The student is questioned by an expert or panel of experts on the subject being evaluated.
- The student takes a written test that has been prepared specifically for the special assessment.
- The student prepares and submits a portfolio providing complete documentation of the knowledge being assessed, and describing how the knowledge was acquired.

Before discussing these various formats, let's look at the steps you should take to make an intelligent decision regarding your ability to earn credits through special assessments. First, a word of caution: special assessments are generally more expensive than any other nontraditional way of earning credits, although they can also be the fastest way to be awarded a large block of credits. Undertake a special assessment only if you are confident of your mastery of the subject and the subject is relevant to your educational goals. Remember, your knowledge must be at least equivalent to that gained through completion of a college course.

Assuming you meet these criteria, the following steps will help prepare you to successfully complete a special assessment.

Step 1: Identify Your Major Learning Experiences. The most efficient and thorough way to identify experiences from which you have learned something of value is to prepare a list of the major or most meaningful experiences of your life. These may be experiences that consumed large amounts of time or energy or that cost you a considerable amount of money. They may have been accomplishments for which you received the formal recognition of others, such as an award, or a great deal of self-satisfaction; or they may simply be experiences from which you know you gained useful knowledge.

Take as much time as you need and make the list as comprehensive as possible. You should enlist the help of friends and relatives who've known you for a long time. They may be able to refresh your memory about experiences you might otherwise overlook. Add every experience of value to the list, no matter how small the learning experience may appear right now. You may later find increased value by combining experiences you might otherwise not list individually. Keep in mind that your success at earning credits through special assessment depends largely on how thorough you are in identifying all possible sources of knowledge.

———

A New Jersey woman succeeded in meeting the requirements for a college degree by earning twenty-five credits through special assessments of the knowledge she gained working with a local theater group, and as a Sunday School teacher at her church. She developed a portfolio detailing her accomplishments as an actress, director, and producer in the theater group. An oral examination of her knowledge of religious education validated that it was equal to that of college-level work. Had she overlooked these experiences she would have had to find another way of earning the credits she needed for her degree.

———

When preparing your list of major learning experiences, be sure to consider all the following examples of experiences through which people usually gain valuable knowledge:

1. Jobs you have had, both full-time and part-time
2. Volunteer work you may have done at the local hospital, church, day-care center, senior citizen center, or animal shelter
3. Participation in a political campaign
4. Hobbies or other leisure-time activities
5. Courses or seminars you've attended
6. Special training you've received, such as first-aid or CPR instruction.

Step 2: Summarize What You Have Learned. Next determine what you learned from each of the experiences or activities on your list. Prepare a separate sheet of paper for each of the experiences you included in step 1. At the top of the page write the experience or activity. Beneath this heading briefly describe everything you believe you learned from the experience or while participating in the activity. This step is as important as the first. You must be as thorough as possible. Remember, it's better to include everything that comes to mind, no matter how trivial it may seem. You can always cross something out later. You may find several items that appear to be limited in the amount of knowledge they provided separately have greater significance when they are linked together. Identifying what you have learned from a particular activity or experience can be difficult, especially when the learning took place in an environment not usually associated with learning, so don't rush through this part of the process. When you run out of things to include, put the list aside and come back to it later.

As you make this list ask yourself these questions:

- What did I have to know to perform this job or duty correctly?
- What have I learned since engaging in this activity?
- Have I developed a special skill from this activity?
- Do people consider me an expert at something?
- Do they seek my advice on problems in a particular field?
- Do I read extensively, especially on particular subjects?

When you feel you've added everything possible to the list under each heading, rewrite each of the descriptions. Explain as fully as possible what you learned, how you learned it, how you may have applied that knowledge to other areas of your life, and what relation that learning may have to a college course. It cannot be overemphasized that this is a time-consuming process that must not be rushed. Keep coming back to it again and again, until you are completely satisfied that you've included every learning experience in your life that may have value toward earning college credits.

Step 3: Make Your Learning Credit Worthy. Next you determine which learning may have some value in earning college credits. Then you can eliminate from your list any that absolutely will not qualify for credit. Don't discard them entirely, because you may later decide one or more can help increase the credit value of other learning experiences.

The following guidelines will help you identify experiential learning that may qualify for college credit. Evaluate each experience against these guidelines and separate your experiences into three categories: those that definitely qualify, those that absolutely do not, and those that fall between.

- You must be able to demonstrate the knowledge either orally, in writing, or in some other visual form, such as artwork or blueprints.
- Your learning must be at least the equal of that normally achieved by undergraduates.
- You must have both a practical and conceptual knowledge of the subject.
- Your knowledge should have a general application and not be applicable solely to the setting or situation in which you acquired it. (An example of what would not qualify for credit is the knowl-

edge of particular procedures that are unique to one company or organization.)
- Your learning should have some demonstrable relationship to an academic field. Some schools may require that it be related to a course of study included in the school's current catalogue.
- A direct relationship between the subject of the special assessment and your *particular* course of study or degree program is a requirement at many schools.

As you progress through this entire process you will find it helpful to review the course catalogues of several different colleges and universities. Course descriptions can help you match your knowledge with what is being taught in a class on the subject. They may also help you describe your knowledge and skills in the terminology used by the college.

Step 4: Document Your Learning. When you request college credit for experiential learning, you are often required to document both the experience and the knowledge or skills gained. This isn't required at all colleges, so you should verify with your school what documentation is required. There are numerous ways to document experiences and accomplishments that translate into learning. The most commonly used are letters of verification, commendations, licenses and permits, samples of your work, certificates, awards and honors, newspaper articles, and written performance evaluations.

When you're accumulating documentation, don't overdo it. Too much documentation can distract the evaluator from an honest assessment of your actual learning. Some evaluators may even suspect heavy documentation as an attempt to cover up weaknesses in your knowledge or skill. If you're using valuable documents such as awards or licenses, submit photocopies, not originals. If a particular document is lengthy, help the evaluator by underlining or highlighting relevant sections or passages.

A popular form of documentation is a letter from a third party attesting to a specific experience and knowledge. The position and status of the person writing such a letter is important in the evaluation process, so select such supporters carefully. When asking someone to write a letter verifying your knowledge and competency, request that they follow these guidelines:

- It should be written on letterhead stationery.
- It must include a description of the writer's present position and pertinent past experience.

- The writer's relationship to you must be clearly identified (e.g., manager), as should the situation in which you were observed and the relevant dates.
- The competencies, knowledge, or skills being attested must be stated specifically.
- Performance evaluations should be made using terms such as average, above average, exceptional, and the like.
- The letter should verify that you held the positions or fulfilled the responsibilities you claim.

When you ask someone to write a letter of verification, be sure he or she understands why you need the letter. You may want to refresh their memory about certain events and discuss your learning experiences with them before they write the letter.

Special Assessment Formats. Most colleges and universities use one of the following formats for assessing experiential learning. Generally you are required to use the format the college has selected, although sometimes the school may give you the option of which format you prefer.

Oral Interview. This is usually a question and answer session between the student and an expert or panel of experts on the subject for which the student is being evaluated. The expert(s) doing the questioning will usually belong to the college faculty. Sometimes the questions are submitted to the student in writing or via an audiotape. In all situations, however, the student is required to respond orally to the questions.

The interview is best suited to the individual who communicates well orally, because the questions asked will require comprehensive answers that demonstrate the breadth and depth of the student's knowledge. If you tend to get stage fright when faced with a questioner, try to get permission to use another method of special assessment.

If you are given the option of which special assessment format to use, here are some of the factors that may influence your decision to use the oral interview: the need to discuss complex concepts, to demonstrate comparisons and conclusions that may require a give-and-take with your questioner, or to translate a foreign language. An oral interview also permits you to demonstrate your self-confidence, a factor that can influence the result of your assessment, particularly if there is a subjective element in the topics you are to discuss.

Written Examination. Two types of examinations are used in special assessments. The first is a straightforward test similar in format to the CLEP examinations discussed in Chapter 7. This form is advantageous to you if your subject knowledge can be easily and fairly tested by multiple-choice questions or by questions requiring short essay answers. The multiple-choice format is used most often for this kind of examination.

If your subject and your knowledge of it require complex answers and explanations of concepts and ideas that can be communicated effectively in writing, an essay examination is often used. This usually consists of several questions or assignments that require you to demonstrate not only your knowledge but also your ability to organize that knowledge into clearly written narratives.

Portfolio Submission. A portfolio is a collection of documents that, as described by the College of New Rochelle, translate your "life experience into a coherent and academically significant document." It must give the college evaluator a complete picture of yourself and of your experiences and the knowledge you've gained from them.

The portfolio submission requirements of each college may vary slightly, but generally your portfolio should be divided into six sections. The first is a signed certification that all the material contained in your portfolio is true and accurate. The second section is a general resume of your life. The third is a listing of the subject areas in which you are seeking credit. Next is a description of the experiences from which you have gained the knowledge now being demonstrated. The fifth section is a description, usually through competency statements, of what you have learned from your experiences. The final section contains the documentation of your experiences and learning we have already discussed.

Whichever format is used for the evaluation of your experiential learning, you are wise to invest as much time as required in your preparation. A well-documented portfolio and a well-written essay on an examination or thoughtful and comprehensive answers to an expert's questions can lead to the award of college credits that can reduce the cost of your degree and save you valuable time.

Policies for Earning Maximum Credits Through Special Assessments. Following is a listing, in alphabetical order by state, of the policies reported by certain colleges and universities concerning the maximum number of credits a student can earn through assessment of experiential learning. Many colleges don't have an established policy, preferring to let each special assessment stand on its own.

NOTE: All credits are reported in semester-hours, unless quarter-hour credits (q) are indicated.

ALABAMA
Athens State College, 96(q); University of Alabama/Birmingham, 64.

ALASKA
Alaska Pacific University, 64; Sheldon Jackson College, 40.

ARIZONA
Embry-Riddle Aeronautical University, 64.

ARKANSAS
University of Arkansas/Monticello, 9.

CALIFORNIA
California State College, Bakersfield, 20; California State University, Chico, 30; California State University, Sacramento, 6; Cogswell College, 18; Dominican College of San Rafael, 12; Humboldt State University, 14; National University, 25; New College of California, 21; Pacific Christian College, 15; University of Redlands, 40; West Coast Christian College, 15.

COLORADO
Loretto Heights College, 98.

CONNECTICUT
Eastern Connecticut State College, 60; Post College, 15; Sacred Heart University, 60; Saint Joseph College, 30; University of Bridgeport, 30; University of Hartford, 60.

DISTRICT OF COLUMBIA
American University, 30; Beacon College, 90; Strayer College, 45(q); Trinity College, 16.

FLORIDA
Barry University, 60; Embry-Riddle Aeronautical University, 64; University of Miami, 6.

GEORGIA
Brenau College, 15(q); Mercer University in Atlanta, 90(q); North Georgia College, 45(q).

HAWAII
Chaminade University of Honolulu, 60.

IDAHO
University of Idaho, 48.

ILLINOIS
Aurora University, 9; Barat College, 30; College of St. Francis, 32; Columbia College, 16; Illinois Benedictine College, 30; National College of Education, 45(q); Southern Illinois University at Carbondale, 30.

INDIANA
Goshen College, 12; Indiana State University, 31; Indiana University at South Bend, 30; Oakland City College, 15; Saint Mary-of-the-Woods College, 30; Saint Meinrad, 24.

IOWA
Briar Cliff College, 30; Buena Vista College, 20; Clarke College, 30; Mount Mercy College, 30; St. Ambrose College, 60; Simpson College, 40; University of Dubuque, 30; Westmar College, 43.

KANSAS
Kansas Newman College, 6; Marymount College of Kansas, 12.

KENTUCKY
Kentucky State University, 17; Morehead State University, 32; Pikeville College, 12; Thomas More College, 60; Union College, 60.

MAINE
University of Maine at Presque Isle, 15; University of Southern Maine, 40.

MARYLAND
Bowie State College, 60; Goucher College, 60; Hood College, 60.

MASSACHUSETTS
Anna Maria College, 6; Babson College, 8; Berkshire Christian College, 15; Bradford College, 6; Elms College, 30; Curry College, 30; Emmanuel College, 16; Nichols College, 30; Simmons College, 24; Southeastern Massachusetts University, 15.

MICHIGAN
Adrian College, 20; Detroit College of Business, 8; Jordan College, 30; Madonna College, 60; Marygrove College, 32; Nazareth College, 30; Sacred Heart Seminary College, 16; St. Mary's College, 30; Siena Heights College, 18; Spring Arbor College, 15.

MINNESOTA
Bemidji State University, 48; College of St. Catherine, 32; College of St. Scholastica, 144(q); College of Saint Teresa, 50(q); Saint Mary's College, 62; Southwest State University, 48(q).

MISSOURI
Central Missouri State University, 30; Columbia College, 45; Fontbonne College, 32; Maryville College–St. Louis, 30; Saint Louis University, 30; Tarkio College, 30.

NEBRASKA
Bellevue College, 36.

NEVADA
Old College, 20.

NEW HAMPSHIRE
Colby-Sawyer College, 24; Daniel Webster College, 30; Hawthorne College, 25.

NEW JERSEY
Bloomfield College, 32; Centenary College, 18; Georgian Court College, 12; Monmouth College, 68; Ramapo College of New Jersey, 75; Saint Peter's College, 30; Upsala College, 32.

NEW MEXICO
College of Santa Fe, 30; College of the Southwest, 30; Eastern New Mexico University, 30.

NEW YORK
Adelphi University, 40; Boricua College, 30; CUNY/Baruch College, 8; CUNY/College of Staten Island, 15; CUNY/Lehman College, 15; CUNY/ John Jay College of Criminal Justice, 32; CUNY/Queens College, 36; CUNY/York College, 32; College of Mount Saint Vincent, 30; College of New Rochelle, 30; Daemen College, 90; Dominican College, 60; Fordham University, 32; Friends World College, 60; Hartwick College, 9; Hobart College, 60; Hofstra University, 30; Long Island University/C. W. Post, 64; Long Island University/Southampton College, 22; Marymount College, 15; Marymount Manhattan College, 30; Medaille College, 60; Mercy College, 15; Mount Saint Mary College, 90; New York Institute of Technology/Old Westbury, 60; New York University, 32; Niagara University, 30; St. Francis College, 30; St. Joseph's College, 27; SUNY College at Buffalo, 30; SUNY College at Fredonia, 15; SUNY College at Old Westbury, 32; SUNY College at Oswego, 40; SUNY Empire State College, 96; Utica College of Syracuse University, 30; William Smith College, 60.

NORTH CAROLINA
Catawba College, 24; High Point College, 12; Mars Hill College, 28; Warren Wilson College, 16; Western Carolina College, 98.

NORTH DAKOTA
Dickinson State College, 48; Mary College, 96.

OHIO
Antioch College, 50; Defiance College, 4; Lake Erie College, 90; Muskingum College, 93; Ohio University, 24; Rio Grande College, 48(q); Tiffin University, 24; Urbana University, 50(q); Ursuline College, 18; Wilmington College, 45(q).

OKLAHOMA
Oklahoma State University, 8.

OREGON
Linfield College, 95; Marylhurst College, 90; Southern Oregon State College, 90(q); Warner Pacific College, 20.

PENNSYLVANIA
Antioch University, 75; Alliance College, 30; Baptist Bible College of Pennsylvania, 18; Bloomsburg University, 64; California University of Pennsylvania, 60; Cedar Crest College, 12; Eastern College, 60; Gwynedd-Mercy College, 60; King's College, 30; Marywood College, 60; Mercyhurst Col-

lege, 6; Point Park College, 30; Rosemont College, 6; Saint Vincent College, 62; University of Scranton, 15; Valley Forge Christian College, 9; Waynesburg College, 15; Wilson College, 15.

SOUTH DAKOTA
Augustana College, 26; Dakota State College, 32; Dakota Wesleyan University, 17; Mount Marty College, 30; Sioux Falls College, 32.

TENNESSEE
Belmont College, 24; Lincoln Memorial College, 45(q); Memphis College of Art, 12; Trevecca Nazarene College, 24(q); Tusculum College, 8; University of Tennessee/Chattanooga, 30; University of Tennessee/Knoxville, 12.

TEXAS
Bishop College, 9; East Texas Baptist College, 30; East Texas State University, 30; Midwestern State University, 18; St. Mary's University of San Antonio, 30; Schreiner College, 30; Southwest Texas State University, 24; Texas A&I University at Kingsville, 42; Texas Christian University, 18.

UTAH
Westminster College, 94.

VERMONT
Burlington College, 90; College of St. Joseph the Provider, 30; Goddard College, 30; Lyndon State College, 90; Norwich University, 60; Trinity College, 90.

VIRGINIA
George Mason University, 4; Virginia Wesleyan College, 30.

WASHINGTON
Cornish Institute, 48; Eastern Washington University, 60; Evergreen State College, 48(q); Pacific Lutheran University, 30; Saint Martin's College, 60.

WEST VIRGINIA
Davis and Elkins College, 31; Wheeling College, 30.

WISCONSIN
Cardinal Stritch College, 36; Mount Mary College, 16; University of Wisconsin/Superior, 144(q).

7

TAKING EXAMINATIONS FOR CREDIT

If you knew that by passing a single examination you could earn the same amount of college credit as if you had taken the course the exam was based on, thereby skipping the course entirely, would you consider taking the exam? Of course you would. Well over one thousand four-year colleges will gladly award you credit for successfully passing certain examinations.

Earning credit by examination has a long and distinguished history. In 1836 the University of London (England) was established solely to award university degrees to candidates based on their performance in a series of examinations.

Today there are over one hundred examinations you can take that, if passed, earn you college credit and entitle you to waive attending the related college course. These tests are known as proficiency examinations because they test your proficiency or knowledge of a given subject. Passing the tests saves you both time and money.

Except for scholarships, proficiency examinations are the most cost-effective method of earning credits that can reduce your cost of earning a college degree. By taking a proficiency examination instead of attending a college class in the same subject you can often reduce your tuition cost by as much as two-thirds. This dramatic savings is enhanced by the elimination of the other costs associated with campus living or commuting to the college during the semester.

The benefits to be derived from taking proficiency examinations are multiplied many times over when we consider the number of colleges and universities that allow you to earn proficiency examination credits equal to 25 percent of the credits required for a bachelor's degree. This means not only a savings in actual expenses, but also a reduction of one full year in the time it will take you to earn your degree. A smaller number of colleges allow up to 50 percent of the required degree credits to be earned through proficiency examinations, cutting your time in college in half.

Later in this chapter (beginning on page 86) there is a list of colleges and universities which award credits for successfully passing proficiency examinations that can reduce the time taken to earn a degree by at least one and in some cases two full years.

Proficiency examinations were originally designed to encourage those outside the education network to pursue a college degree. These were usually adults who couldn't attend traditional college classes because of work or child-rearing responsibilities. Now high school graduates entering colleges are taking advantage of these examination programs to reduce their expenses and the time it takes them to earn their degrees. Most colleges and universities accept credits earned through proficiency examinations in place of class attendance. While the grade criteria and number of credits applicable to a degree vary widely among colleges, the substantial amount of time and money you can save make this a worthwhile route.

The Examination Programs. While some colleges develop their own examinations, the two most widely used and accepted proficiency examination programs are the College Level Examination Program (CLEP) and the Proficiency Examination Program (PEP). Credits earned through either of these programs can be applied toward a bachelor's degree at most American colleges and universities.

CLEP is sponsored by the College Board. The examinations, which are administered by the Educational Testing Service, are given regularly at over one thousand locations in the United States.

PEP is sponsored and administered by the American College Testing Program. The tests are given six times each year at over one hundred locations throughout the country.

What the Examinations Test. There are two types of CLEP examinations: specific subject and general. The five general examinations are the most popular, in part because they test areas of knowledge usually referred to as "general education" that are required of most college students. The five areas covered are English composition, mathematics, natural sciences, humanities, and social sciences. Each examination has a 90-minute time limit and consists entirely of multiple-choice questions that measure intellectual experience instead of specific knowledge. While each of the five can be taken individually, together they represent the core of a liberal arts education for freshmen and sophomores.

The CLEP subject examinations are available to test specific knowledge in 45 subjects. They are comparable to the examination you would take at the completion of a college course. Most subject examinations are also in the multiple-choice format, with the same 90-minute time limit as the general examinations. Many also have an optional 90-minute essay portion that some colleges require before awarding you credit. Be sure you know if this essay portion is required by your college before taking the examination.

Each of the PEP examinations covers a specific subject. Most are composed entirely of multiple-choice questions, although some combine these with an essay, or free-response, question. Students taking a PEP examination are generally given up to three hours to complete the test. PEP examines both your knowledge of a particular subject and your ability to apply its concepts.

How You Earn Credit. Neither the College Board nor the American College Testing Program award college credit. The credit you receive for passing the proficiency examinations is awarded by the college you are attending. Each college decides on which examinations it will award credit, what minimum score is acceptable as a passing grade, and how much credit is awarded. Because of the popularity of proficiency examination programs, these policies are probably already determined in the college you are attending or plan to attend. Before you take any proficiency examination be sure you understand your college's policy concerning the examination.

When you take a proficiency examination, you will be asked to whom you want the results sent beside yourself. Fill in the name of your college, and the results will be sent to both the college and you, usually in about six weeks.

Subjects Tested and Credit Awarded. Following is a listing of the subjects for which you can take either CLEP or PEP proficiency examinations. The number following each subject is the amount of college credit that is generally awarded for achieving a passing score. Use this number only as a general guide. Remember that it is your college alone that determines both the passing score and the amount of credit to be awarded. Students passing the CLEP General

Examinations are usually awarded six semester credits for each of the five examinations.

CLEP examinations are available in the following subjects:

Business. Computers and data processing (4); elementary computer programming (3); introduction to business management (3); introductory accounting (4); introductory business law (3); introductory marketing (3); money and banking (3).

Dental Auxiliary Education. Dental materials (3); head, neck, and oral anatomy (3); oral radiography (3); tooth morphology and function (3).

Education. Educational psychology (3); history of American education (3); human growth and development (3); tests and measurements (3).

Humanities. American literature (6); analysis and interpretation of literature (6); college composition (6); college French, levels 1 and 2 (12); college German, levels 1 and 2 (12); college Spanish, levels 1 and 2 (12); English literature (6); freshman literature (6).

Mathematics. Calculus with elementary functions (6); college algebra (3); college algebra-trigonometry (3); statistics (3); trigonometry (3).

Medical Technology. Clinical chemistry (6); hematology (6); immunohematology and blood banking (6); microbiology (3).

Nursing. Anatomy, physiology, microbiology (6); behavioral sciences for nurses (6); fundamentals of nursing (6); medical-surgical nursing (6).

Sciences. General biology (6); general chemistry (6).

Social Sciences. Afro-American history (3); American government (3); American history (6); general psychology (3); introductory macroeconomics (3); introductory microeconomics (3); introductory micro- and macroeconomics (6); introductory sociology (6); Western civilization (6).

PEP examinations are available in the following subjects:

Arts and Sciences:. African and Afro-American history (6); anatomy and physiology (6); earth sciences (6); freshman English (6); Shakespeare (3).

Business. Accounting, level I (6); accounting, level II (9); accounting, level III, area I (12); accounting, level III, area II (12); accounting, level III, area III (12); finance, level I (9); finance, level II (9); finance, level III (12); management of human resources, level I (6); management of human resources, level II (9); management of human resources, level III (12); marketing, level I (3); marketing, level II (9); marketing, level III (12); operations management, level I (9); operations management, level II (9); operations management, level III (12); business environment and strategy (6).

Criminal Justice. Introduction to criminal justice (3); criminal investigation (3).

Education. Educational psychology (3); history of American education (3); reading instruction in the elementary school (6); corrective and remedial instruction in reading (9).

Nursing. Fundamentals of nursing (8); maternal and child nursing (12); adult nursing (12); psychiatric/mental health nursing (6); commonalities in nursing care, area I (4); commonalities in nursing care, area II (4); health support, area I (4); health support, area II (4); differences in nursing care, area I (4); differences in nursing care, area II (4); differences in nursing care, area III (4); nursing health care (4); occupational strategy nursing (4); professional strategies, nursing (4).

What the Examinations Cost. The current charge for taking a CLEP examination is $35. The charge for most PEP examinations is between $35 and $50. Compare those charges to the tuition a college charges for taking comparable courses and you can quickly see the amount of money you will save by taking proficiency examinations.

One note of warning on expenses. Some colleges charge a small fee for processing your proficiency examination credits. Under no circumstances should you permit the college to charge you anything other than this small processing fee. In rare cases in the past a few colleges have attempted to charge students a fee equal to the amount they charge for the course the student is skipping because of passing a proficiency examination. The tuition a student pays for participation in a class is supposed to help cover the costs and overhead of operating that class and should not be charged to students not taking the class. Find out what your college's policy is before deciding to take a proficiency examination or before you enroll in a college with such an unethical policy.

Selecting the Right Examinations. Before taking any proficiency examination discuss your plans with the appropriate official of your college. This might be a student advisor or the head of the department in which you're enrolled. Make sure you have been given official permission to take the examination and that the college will award you credit for achieving a passing grade.

Preparing for the Examinations. Once you've selected a proficiency examination you must begin the preparations that can help you score high enough to be awarded the credits you want. Proper preparation is the key to passing any examination.

The best place to start is at your local library. Nearly a dozen publishers currently publish books designed to help you score high on both the CLEP and PEP examinations. Most contain samples of questions from earlier tests, and offer advice on what books to read as part of your preparation. Among the best of these is published by the College Board for those taking CLEP examinations. *The College Board Guide to the CLEP Examinations* is called "the official guide." It contains over one hundred questions from the general examinations, over 750 from the subject examinations, and complete descriptions of each test. If you can't find this book in your library, you can order your own copy from College Board Publications, Box 886, New York, NY 10101-0886.

The American College Testing Program publishes its own *Proficiency Examination Study Guide* for each PEP examination. Each of these guides provides you with the objective of the examination, usually in terms of what you should be able to demonstrate through your performance on the test. Each also includes an in-depth description of the examination content, an indication of how much emphasis is placed on each area within the subject, and a list of the books and other materials used in developing the examination. These guides are available at no charge from ACT-PEP Coordinator, Proficiency Examination Program, P.O. Box 168, Iowa City, IA 52243.

Saving a Year Through Proficiency Examinations. The following colleges and universities will award approximately 25 percent of the total credits required for a bachelor's degree upon successful completion of proficiency examinations. This means that by meeting the grade and test requirements you can save the expenses involved in attending college for one full year. Contact those colleges in which you are interested to learn the minimum acceptable grades and the examinations that qualify. Those colleges whose names are preceded by an asterisk (*) are willing to award 50 percent or more of the credits required to earn a degree through examinations. The colleges and universities listed below can be found in the Appendix, *College Profiles for Cost Cutters.*

ALABAMA
*Athens State College; *Birmingham–Southern College; Faulkner University; Huntingdon College; Jacksonville State University; Judson College; Livingston University; Oakwood College; Samford University; Spring Hill College; *Troy State University (all campuses); University of Alabama; *University of Alabama/Birmingham; University of Alabama/Huntsville; University of Montevallo; University of North Alabama; University of South Alabama.

ALASKA
Alaska Pacific University; Sheldon Jackson College; University of Alaska/ Juneau.

ARIZONA
Arizona State University; Grand Canyon College; Northern Arizona University; Southwestern Baptist Bible College; *University of Arizona.

ARKANSAS
Arkansas College; Arkansas State University; Arkansas Tech University; College of the Ozarks; Harding University; Henderson State University; Hendrix College; Ouachita Baptist University; Southern Arkansas University; University of Arkansas at Little Rock; University of Arkansas at Monticello; University of Central Arkansas.

CALIFORNIA
Art Center College of Design; Biola University; California Baptist College; California Polytechnic State University; California State University/Chico; California State University/Dominguez Hills; California State University/ Fresno; California State University/Fullerton; California State University/ Hayward; California State University/Sacramento; Chapman College; College of Notre Dame; Humphreys College; Monterey Institute of International Studies; Mount St. Mary's College; Pacific Christian College; Pacific Union College; Pepperdine University; Point Loma College; Pomona College; Saint Mary's College of California; San Diego State University; San Francisco State University; San Jose State University; Sonoma State University; Stanford University; United States International University; University of La Verne; University of Southern California; Whittier College.

COLORADO
Adams State College; Colorado State University; Loretto Heights College; Mesa College; *Metropolitan State College; Regis College; University of Colorado/Boulder; University of Colorado/Colorado Springs; University of Colorado/Denver; University of Denver; University of Northern Colorado; Western State College of Colorado.

CONNECTICUT
Albertus Magnus College; Central Connecticut State University; *Eastern Connecticut State College; Fairfield University; Quinnipiac College; *Sacred

Heart University; Saint Joseph College; University of Bridgeport; University of Connecticut; *Western Connecticut State University.

DELAWARE
Wesley College; *Widener University.

DISTRICT OF COLUMBIA
American University; *Beacon College; George Washington University; *Howard University; Mount Vernon College; Strayer College.

FLORIDA
Baptist Bible Institute; Barry University; Bethune-Cookman College; College of Boca Raton; *Eckerd College; Flagler College; Florida A&M University; Florida Atlantic University; Florida International University; *Florida Southern College; *Florida State University; *Jacksonville University; *Miami Christian College; *Nova University; Palm Beach Atlantic College; Rollins College; Saint John Vianney College Seminary; Saint Leo College; Saint Thomas University; Southeastern College of the Assemblies of God; *Stetson University; University of Central Florida; University of Florida; *University of Miami; *University of North Florida; University of South Florida; *University of Tampa; University of West Florida; Webber College.

GEORGIA
Albany State College; *Armstrong State College; Augusta State College; Berry College; Breneau College; *Columbus College; Covenant College; Fort Valley State College; Georgia College; Georgia Southern College; Georgia Southwestern College; Kennesaw College; LaGrange College; Mercer University; *Mercer University in Atlanta; Morris Brown College; North Georgia College; Oglethorpe University; Piedmont College; Savannah State College; *Spelman College; *Tift College; Toccoa Falls College; Valdosta State College; West Georgia College.

HAWAII
*Chaminade University of Honolulu; Hawaii Pacific College; University of Hawaii at Hilo.

IDAHO
*Boise State University; *College of Idaho; Idaho State University; Northwest Nazarene College; University of Idaho.

ILLINOIS
*Aurora University; Barat College; Blackburn College; *Bradley University; *Chicago State University; College of St. Francis; *Columbia College; *DePaul University; *Illinois College; MacMurray College; McKendree College; National College of Education; North Central College; Northeastern Illinois University; *North Park College; Parks College of St. Louis University; Quincy College; *Rockford College; Southern Illinois University at Carbondale; Trinity Christian College; *Trinity College; University of Illinois at Chicago; Western Illinois University; Wheaton College.

INDIANA

Anderson College; *Ball State University; *Calumet College; DePauw University; Fort Wayne Bible College; Franklin College of Indiana; Huntington College; Indiana State University; *Indiana University/Kokomo; *Indiana University/South Bend; Oakland City College; *Saint Francis College; Saint Joseph's College; Saint Mary's College; *University of Evansville.

IOWA

Briar Cliff College; Clark College; Iowa Wesleyan College; Loras College; Morningside College; Mount Mercy College; Mount Saint Clare College; *St. Ambrose College; University of Iowa; University of Northern Iowa; Westmar College.

KANSAS

Benedictine College; Bethany College; Emporia State University; Friends University; Kansas Newman College; *Marymount College of Kansas; Southwestern College; Sterling College; University of Kansas; Washburn University of Topeka.

KENTUCKY

Asbury College; Brescia College; Campbellsville College; Cumberland College; *Kentucky State University; Kentucky Wesleyan College; Morehead State University; Murray State University; Northern Kentucky University; Pikeville College; Spalding University; Thomas More College; Union College; *University of Kentucky.

LOUISIANA

Dillard University; Louisiana State University and A&M College; *Louisiana State University; *Louisiana Tech University; Loyola University; McNeese State University; *Nicholls State University; *Our Lady of Holy Cross College; *Southeastern Louisiana University; University of Southwestern Louisiana; Xavier University of Louisiana.

MAINE

College of the Atlantic; Husson College; *Thomas College; University of Maine at Farmington; *University of Maine at Kent; *University of Maine at Orono; *University of Maine at Presque Isle; University of New England.

MARYLAND

*Bowie State College; *Capitol Institute of Technology; Coppin State College; Frostburg State College; Goucher College; Hood College; Loyola College; Maryland Institute College of Art; Mount Saint Mary's College; *St. Mary's College of Maryland; *Salisbury State College; Towson State University; *University of Maryland at College Park; *University of Maryland/Baltimore County; *University of Maryland/Eastern Shore; Washington College; Western Maryland College.

MASSACHUSETTS

*American International College; Anna Maria College; Assumption College; Atlantic Union College; *Babson College; Bentley College; Berkshire Christian College; Boston University; Elms College; *Curry College; Emerson College; Emmanuel College; *Fitchburg State College; *Framingham State College; *Merrimack College; Nichols College; *Northeastern University; Southeastern Massachusetts University; Springfield College; Stonehill College; *Suffolk University; University of Lowell; *Western New England College; *Westfield State College; Wheelock College; Worcester State College.

MICHIGAN
Adrian College; Albion College; Andrews University; *Cleary College; Detroit College of Business; Eastern Michigan University; Grand Rapids Baptist College; Hope College; Jordan College; Lake Superior State College; Madonna College; Marygrove College; Mercy College of Detroit; Michigan Christian College; Michigan State University; Nazareth College; Northern Michigan University; *Oakland University; *Saginaw Valley State College; St. Mary's College; Siena Heights College; *Spring Arbor College; University of Detroit; Wayne State University.

MINNESOTA
Augsburg College; College of St. Catherine; College of St. Scholastica; College of Saint Teresa; Hamline University; North Central Bible College; St. Cloud State University; Saint Mary's College; *St. Paul Bible College; Southwest State University; *University of Minnesota/Duluth; University of Minnesota/Morris.

MISSISSIPPI
Blue Mountain College; Delta State University; Jackson State University; Mississippi State University; Mississippi University for Women; *University of Mississippi; University of Southern Mississippi; William Carey College.

MISSOURI
Central Methodist College; Central Missouri State University; *Columbia College; Drury College; Evangel College; Fontbonne College; Hannibal-LaGrange College; Lincoln University; Maryville College–St. Louis; Missouri Baptist College; Missouri Valley College; Missouri Western State College; Northwest Missouri State University; Rockhurst College; Saint Louis Conservatory of Music; Saint Louis University; School of the Ozarks; Southeast Missouri State University; Southwest Missouri State University; University of Missouri/Kansas City; *University of Missouri/Rolla; University of Missouri/St. Louis; Westminster College; William Jewell College; William Woods College.

MONTANA
College of Great Falls; Montana College of Mineral Science and Technology; Northern Montana College; Rocky Mountain College.

NEBRASKA
Bellevue College; *Chadron State College; Dana College; Midland Lutheran College; Union College.

NEVADA
Sierra Nevada College; University of Nevada/Las Vegas; *University of Las Vegas/Reno.

NEW HAMPSHIRE
*Colby-Sawyer College; Daniel Webster College; Franklin Pierce College; Keene State College; *New Hampshire College; Plymouth State College; *Rivier College; *University of New Hampshire.

NEW JERSEY
*Bloomfield College; Caldwell College; Centenary College; College of Saint Elizabeth; Drew University; *Fairleigh Dickinson University (all campuses); Felician College; Georgian Court College; Glassboro State College; Monmouth College; *Montclair State College; Northeastern Bible College; Princeton University; *Ramapo College of New Jersey; Saint Peter's College; Seton Hall University; *Trenton State College; Upsala College; *William Paterson College of New Jersey.

NEW MEXICO
College of Santa Fe; College of the Southwest; Eastern New Mexico University; New Mexico State University; University of New Mexico; Western New Mexico University.

NEW YORK
Adelphi University; Boricua College; Canisius College; CUNY/Bernard Baruch College; CUNY/College of Staten Island; CUNY/Herbert Lehman College; CUNY/John Jay College of Criminal Justice; CUNY/Medgar Evers College; CUNY/York College; *Colgate University; *Daemen College; *Dominican College; *Dowling College; D'Youville College; Elmira College; Fordham University; *Friends World College; Hartwick College; Hofstra University; Houghton College; *Iona College; King's College; *Le Moyne College; *Long Island University (all campuses); Manhattan College; Marymount College; Marymount Manhattan College; Molloy College; Nazareth College of Rochester; *New York Institute of Technology/Old Westbury; New York University; Niagara University; Pace University, College of White Plains; Pratt Institute; Roberts Wesleyan College; *Russell Sage College; *St. Francis College; *St. John Fisher College; St. Joseph's College; St. Joseph's College/Suffolk; St. Thomas Aquinas College; *SUNY at Albany; SUNY College at Buffalo; SUNY College at Fredonia; SUNY College at Geneseo; SUNY College at New Paltz; SUNY College at Oneonta; SUNY College at Oswego; SUNY College at Plattsburgh; SUNY College at Potsdam; SUNY College at Purchase; SUNY College of Technology at Utica; *SUNY Empire State College; Utica College of Syracuse University; Wadhams Hall Seminary-College; Wagner College.

NORTH CAROLINA
Atlantic Christian College; Belmont Abbey College; *Bennett College; Campbell University; East Carolina University; Fayetteville State University; Gardner-Webb College; Guilford College; High Point College; Mars Hill College; *Methodist College; Mount Olive College; Pembroke State University; Queens College; Sacred Heart College; St. Andrews Presbyterian College; University of North Carolina/Asheville; University of North Carolina/Charlotte; *University of North Carolina/Greensboro; *Wake Forest Univer-

sity; *Western Carolina University; Wingate College; Winston-Salem State University.

NORTH DAKOTA
Dickinson State College; *Mary College; Minot State College; Valley City State College.

OHIO
Ashland College; Bowling Green State University; *College of Mount St. Joseph on the Ohio; Findlay College; *Franklin University; Heidelberg College; *Hiram College; John Carroll University; *Lake Erie College; *Malone College; Marietta College; Miami University; Mount Vernon Nazarene College; Ohio Northern University; Ohio State University; Ohio University; Otterbein College; Pontifical College Josephinum; Tiffin University; University of Dayton; University of Steubenville; University of Toledo; Ursuline College; Walsh College; Wilberforce University; Wilmington College.

OKLAHOMA
Bartlesville Wesleyan College; Bethany Nazarene College; *Cameron University; *East Central University; *Northwestern Oklahoma State University; Oklahoma Baptist University; *Oklahoma Christian College; *Oklahoma City University; Oklahoma State University; Southeastern Oklahoma State University; *Southwestern Oklahoma State University; *University of Oklahoma; *University of Science and Arts of Oklahoma.

OREGON
Eastern Oregon State College; *George Fox College; Lewis and Clark College; Linfield College; *Oregon State University; Reed College; Western Baptist College; Western Oregon State University.

PENNSYLVANIA
*Allentown College of St. Francis de Sales; *Alliance College; Alvernia College; *Beaver College; *Bloomsburg University; Bucknell University; *Cabrini College; *California University of Pennsylvania; *Cedar Crest College; Clarion University; College Misericordia; Drexel University; *Duquesne University; *Eastern College; Edinboro University; Elizabethtown College; Franklin and Marshall College; Gannon University; Geneva College; *Gwynedd-Mercy College; Holy Family College; *Immaculata College; King's College; *LaRoche College; *LaSalle University; Lock Haven University; *Lycoming College; Marywood College; Mercyhurst College; *Millersville University; *Muhlenberg College; Neumann College; *Pennsylvania State University; *Philadelphia College of Textiles and Science; *Point Park College; Robert Morris College; Saint Francis College; *Saint Vincent College; Seton Hill College; Shippensburg University; Slippery Rock University; *Temple University; *Thiel College; University of Pittsburgh at Bradford; University of Scranton; Ursinus College; Valley Forge Christian College; Villa Maria College; *Washington and Jefferson College; West Chester University; *Widener University; *York College of Pennsylvania.

RHODE ISLAND
Barrington College; Bryant College; Providence College; *Rhode Island College; Roger Williams College; *University of Rhode Island.

SOUTH CAROLINA
Baptist College at Charleston; The Citadel; College of Charleston; Converse College; Lander College; *Limestone College; Newberry College; University of South Carolina at Aiken; University of South Carolina at Spartanburg; *University of South Carolina, Coastal Carolina College; Winthrop College; Wofford College.

SOUTH DAKOTA
Augustana College; Black Hills State College; Dakota State College; Mount Marty College; *National College; Sioux Falls College; South Dakota State University; University of South Dakota.

TENNESSEE
*Austin Peay State University; Bethel College; Bryan College; Christian Brothers College; David Lipscomb College; Fisk University; Freed-Hardeman College; King College; Lambuth College; Lee College; LeMoyne-Owen College; Lincoln Memorial University; Maryville College; *Middle Tennessee State University; Southern College of Seventh-Day Adventists; Tennessee Technological University; Tennessee Temple University; Trevecca Nazarene College; Tusculum College; Union University; University of Tennessee at Chattanooga; University of Tennessee at Martin.

TEXAS
Abilene Christian University; *Baylor University; Concordia Lutheran College; East Texas Baptist College; Hardin-Simmons University; Howard Payne University; Lubbock Christian College; McMurry College; Midwestern State University; Prairie View A&M University; St. Mary's University of San Antonio; Sul Ross State University; Texas Southern University; Texas Wesleyan College; Texas Women's University; Trinity University; University of Dallas; University of Texas at Arlington; University of Texas at Austin.

UTAH
Southern Utah State College; University of Utah; Weber State College; Westminster College.

VERMONT
*Burlington College; *Castleton State College; Goddard College; *Green Mountain College; *Lyndon State College; Saint Michael's College; Trinity College.

VIRGINIA
*Christopher Newport College; George Mason University; James Madison University; Norfolk State University; Old Dominion University; Radford University; Randolph-Macon Women's College; Shenandoah College and Conservatory; University of Richmond; Virginia Commonwealth University; Virginia Wesleyan College.

WASHINGTON

Gonzaga University; *Griffin College; Pacific Lutheran University; *Saint Martin's College; Seattle Pacific University; Seattle University; University of Puget Sound; *Washington State University; Western Washington University; Whitworth College.

WEST VIRGINIA

*Alderson-Broaddus College; Davis and Elkins College; Salem College; Shepherd College; *University of Charleston; *West Virginia Institute of Technology; West Virginia Wesleyan College; *Wheeling College.

WISCONSIN

Beloit College; *Cardinal Stritch College; *Carroll College; Carthage College; Marquette University; *St. Norbert College; Silver Lake College; University of Wisconsin/Eau Claire; University of Wisconsin/La Crosse; University of Wisconsin/Oshkosh; University of Wisconsin/Parkside; University of Wisconsin/Platteville; University of Wisconsin/Stevens Point; University of Wisconsin/Superior; *University of Wisconsin/Whitewater.

8

HOW TO GET A HEAD START

In this chapter we'll look at several programs that permit bright and industrious high school students to reduce the time it will take them to earn a college degree by as much as one year. These programs aren't for the average student, but are for those who are highly motivated to obtain a higher education.

High school students who want to get a head start on a college education must start planning during their junior year or even earlier.

Advanced Placement. In the early 1950s the Fund for the Advancement of Education of the Ford Foundation sponsored two independent projects that resulted in what today is known as the Advanced Placement Program. This is a program that makes it possible for college-bound high school students to cut the time it will take them to earn a college degree by as much as one year.

The first of these two projects, known as the School and College Study of General Education, addressed the problems that resulted in many well-prepared students studying essentially the same material during their first year in college that they did in their senior high school year. The project report recommended: "What is needed is a set of achievement examinations in the major subjects taught in secondary schools which would enable the colleges . . . to give an entering student advanced placement . . ."

The second project, the Kenyon Plan, was a cooperative effort of twelve colleges, several high schools, and the Educational Testing Service in developing courses and tests that resulted in entering freshmen receiving advanced placement in selected subjects. In 1955 the program became the responsibility of the College Entrance Examination Board and has since been known as the Advanced Placement Program, or simply AP.

AP permits you, as a high school student, to receive credit for college courses without actually taking them. AP is an excellent method for cutting your college costs by as much as 25 percent, because it's possible for you to earn enough credits to enter college as a sophomore instead of a freshman, thus saving an entire year.

Those readers who are long past the age of high school and are interested in how adults can make use of AP exams to earn college credits should turn to Chapter 11.

———

When Anthony Alvarez entered Stanford University, he was awarded 15 credits, the equivalent of a full quarter, based on the five AP examinations he took during his last two years at Los Angeles's Garfield High School.

———

Almost every college in the United States and many in other countries make some use of AP examinations. Approximately 1,200 American colleges are prepared to offer you as much as one full year's credit and placement based on your presentation of enough qualifying AP grades.

Advanced Placement is a two-part program: the first part is a course taught at the student's high school; the second is a test based on the material covered in an AP course. The test is graded and the grade sent to the college of the student's choice.

The AP Courses. There are currently 26 AP courses available. Each usually runs a full academic year. Students attending these courses should be prepared for college-level work that is substantially more demanding than many of the high school courses they've been taking. In some of the over 7,000 high schools that participate in AP, the course is known as the AP course. In others, it may be an honors class, a tutorial, or even a strong regular class. Students attending schools not offering AP examination preparation courses can participate in the program through independent study.

Whichever approach you take, you're sure to find AP course work a stimulating experience. It can also help prepare you for college courses.

———

Pearletha Phillips, who received credit from Princeton for her AP grades, describes how she feels about the AP courses she took: "I cannot honestly tell you that AP courses are easy. They are *not.* They are so different from most high school courses that it is not unusual for a student to experience a certain period of culture shock."

———

The AP Examinations. The AP courses help prepare you for the AP examinations. It is through these examinations that you can earn enough credits to qualify you to enter college as a sophomore. If your high school doesn't participate in the AP program, or if you are not attending high school, you can contact the program administrators for a list of participating high schools in your area. The address and telephone number is:

> AP Services
> P.O. Box 6671
> Princeton, NJ 08541-6671
> (215) 750-8300

Once you've identified a participating high school find out who the AP coordinator is for the school and arrange with that person to take the examinations.

Each AP examination costs $53. That's money well spent when you weigh that amount against what it costs to take one course at a nearby college. The College Board describes the exams as "tough but fair." With some variations the exams are composed of multiple-choice and free-response questions. The former give you several possible answers to choose from, while the latter require use of problem-solving and essay-writing skills.

The examinations are given once each year, in May. The scores are reported in July and sent to the college(s) you designate. If you want to participate in the AP examination program, you must contact a high school AP coordinator in the early part of February.

The Subjects Covered. AP courses and examinations are currently available for the following subjects: history of art; studio art; biology; chemistry; computer science; English language and composition; English literature and composition; French language, level 3; French literature, level 3; German language, level 3; American government and politics; comparative government and politics; American history; European history; Vergil (Latin); Catullus-Horace (Latin); calculus AB; calculus BC; music: listening and literature; theory of music; physics B; mechanics (physics C); electricity and magnetism (physics C); Spanish language, level 3; and Spanish literature, level 3.

Grades and College Credits. The AP examinations are graded according to the following scale:

5   extremely well qualified

4   well qualified

3   qualified

2   possibly qualified

1   no recommendation

It's up to your college which grade level will be accepted for credit. Neither the College Board nor the Educational Testing Service, which administers the examinations, grants credit. The college will notify you how much credit you've earned after an evaluation of your examination results.

To learn which colleges award credit for passing the AP examinations, see the Appendix, *College Profiles for Cost Cutters*. In addition, the last portion of this chapter contains a list of those colleges and universities that grant sophomore standing to entering students with qualifying grades in enough AP examinations.

Advanced Standing. Not to be confused with AP, advanced standing programs are usually designed to allow especially bright high school students to earn academic credits by attending regular college classes during their last year in high school. These classes are intended to help prepare industrious and capable high school students for the college experience and reduce the time needed to earn their degrees.

Advanced standing programs that are given in summer session allow students to attend classes at the college during the summers before and following their senior high school year. The classes are given for full credit and count toward the total number of credits the student needs to earn a degree.

By using advanced standing programs it's possible for a high school senior to accumulate enough credits to reduce the time that will have to be spent in college to earn a degree by as much as one semester.

Early Admission. Some colleges allow high school juniors with outstanding records or those attending schools with rigorous curricula to apply for admission before their senior year. This means a student who succeeds in gaining early admission will skip the senior year in high school completely. The general practice in such cases is to award the student a high school diploma on completion of the freshman year of college. The net result is college entry and graduation one year early. Although the direct financial benefits of early admission are small, the long-term benefits make it worthwhile for those who can qualify. Admissions standards are more stringent for early admission applicants than for traditional applicants. Because of the seriousness of skipping the senior year of high school, college admissions officials are especially interested in the emotional maturity and academic abilities of early admission applicants.

To learn if the colleges you are interested in attending participate in either advanced standing or early admission programs, review their catalogues.

Correspondence Courses. Many of the colleges and universities that offer correspondence courses for academic credit will permit high school students to earn credits this way before graduation. Most place no limit on the number of these courses a high school student can take. If you are a high school student willing to do the work required for successful completion of a correspondence course, you can begin earning college credits before entering college. For more information see Chapter 5.

Colleges That Award Sophomore Standing Through the AP Examination Program. The following colleges and universities award credit equal to one full year for successfully passing AP examinations. Each college sets its own policy concerning the examinations it recognizes and the grades it considers acceptable, so you must contact each college you are interested in attending for more specific information.

ALABAMA
Alabama A&M University; Birmingham–Southern University; Faulkner University; Livingston University; Samford University; University of Alabama/Birmingham; University of Montevallo; University of North Alabama; University of South Alabama.

ALASKA
Alaska Pacific University; University of Alaska/Fairbanks; University of Alaska/Juneau.

ARKANSAS
Hendrix College; University of Central Arkansas.

CALIFORNIA

California Baptist College; California Institute of the Arts; California Lutheran University; California State College, Bakersfield; California State Polytechnic University; California State University (all campuses); Chapman College; Claremont McKenna College; College of Notre Dame; Fresno Pacific College; Golden Gate University; Harvey Mudd College; Holy Names College; Humboldt State University; Loyola Marymount University; Menlo College; Mills College; Mount St. Mary's College; New College of California; Pacific Union College; Pitzer College; Point Loma College; Saint Mary's College of California; San Francisco State University; San Jose State University; Simpson College; Sonoma State University; Southern California College; Stanford University; United States International University; University of California (all campuses); University of La Verne; University of San Diego; University of San Francisco; University of Southern California; University of the Pacific; West Coast University; Westmont College; Whittier College; Woodbury University.

COLORADO

Adams State College; Colorado College; Colorado School of Mines; Colorado State University; Colorado Technical College; Fort Lewis College; Metropolitan State College; University of Colorado (all campuses); University of Denver; University of Northern Colorado.

CONNECTICUT

Connecticut College; Eastern Connecticut State University; Quinnipiac College; Sacred Heart University; Saint Joseph College; Trinity College; University of Bridgeport; University of Connecticut; University of New Haven; Wesleyan University; Western Connecticut State University; Yale University.

DELAWARE

University of Delaware; Widener University; Wilmington College.

DISTRICT OF COLUMBIA

American University; Catholic University of America; George Washington University; Howard University; Mount Vernon College; Trinity College.

FLORIDA

Barry University; Bethune-Cookman College; College of Boca Raton; Eckerd College; Embry-Riddle Aeronautical University; Flagler College; Florida A&M University; Florida International University; Florida Southern College; Florida State University; Jacksonville University; Miami Christian College; Nova University; Orlando College; Saint Leo College; Saint Thomas University; Stetson University; University of Central Florida; University of Florida; University of Miami; University of Tampa.

GEORGIA

Agnes Scott College; Berry College; Brenau College; Columbus College; Covenant College; Emory University; Georgia College; Georgia Institute of Technology; Georgia Southern College; Georgia State University; Kennesaw College; LaGrange College; Mercer University; Mercer University/Atlanta;

Oglethorpe University; Piedmont College; Toccoa Falls College; University of Georgia; Valdosta State College; West Georgia College.

HAWAII
Hawaii Loa College; University of Hawaii/Hilo; University of Hawaii/Manoa.

IDAHO
Boise State University; College of Idaho; Idaho State University; Northwest Nazarene College; University of Idaho.

ILLINOIS
Augustana College; Aurora University; Blackburn College; Bradley University; Chicago State University; College of St. Francis; DePaul University; Eastern Illinois University; Elmhurst College; Illinois Benedictine College; Illinois College; Illinois State University; Illinois Wesleyan University; Judson College; Knox College; Lake Forest College; Lewis University; Loyola University of Chicago; MacMurray College; McKendree College; Millikin University; Mundelein College; North Park College; Northeastern Illinois University; Northern Illinois University; Northwestern University; Parks College of St. Louis University; Quincy College; Roosevelt University; Rosary College; Southern Illinois University at Carbondale; Spertus College of Judaica; Trinity Christian College; University of Illinois at Chicago; Western Illinois University; Wheaton College.

INDIANA
Ball State University; Butler University; DePauw University; Franklin College of Indiana; Grace College; Huntington College; Indiana Institute of Technology; Indiana State University; Indiana University; Indiana University/Kokomo; Indiana University/Northwest; Marion College; Oakland City College; Purdue University; Purdue University/North Central; Saint Francis College; Saint Joseph's College; Saint Mary-of-the-Woods College; Saint Mary's College; University of Evansville; University of Southern Indiana; Valparaiso University; Wabash College.

IOWA
Briar Cliff College; Central University of Iowa; Clarke College; Cornell College; Drake University; Graceland College; Iowa State University; Iowa Wesleyan College; Morningside College; Mount Mercy College; Northwestern College; St. Ambrose College; Simpson College; University of Iowa; Wartburg College; Westmar College.

KANSAS
Baker University; Benedictine College; Bethany College; Bethel College; Emporia State University; Fort Hays State University; Kansas State University; Marymount College of Kansas; Mid-America Nazarene College; Pittsburg State University; Tabor College; University of Kansas.

KENTUCKY
Asbury College; Bellarmine College; Campbellsville College; Cumberland College; Eastern Kentucky University; Georgetown College; Kentucky Wes-

leyan College; Morehead State University; Murray State University; Northern Kentucky University; Pikeville College; Spalding University; Thomas More College; University of Kentucky; Western Kentucky University.

LOUISIANA
Centenary College of Louisiana; Dillard University; Louisiana State University and A&M College; Loyola University; McNeese State University; Northwestern State University; Southeastern Louisiana University; Tulane University/Newcomb College; Xavier University of Louisiana.

MAINE
Bates College; Bowdoin College; Colby College; College of the Atlantic; Thomas College; Unity College; University of Maine (all campuses); University of Southern Maine; Westbrook College.

MARYLAND
Bowie State College; College of Notre Dame of Maryland; Frostburg State College; Hood College; Johns Hopkins University; Loyola College; Mount Saint Mary's College; St. Mary's College of Maryland; Salisbury State College; Towson State University; University of Maryland (all campuses); Washington College; Western Maryland College.

MASSACHUSETTS
American International College; Anna Maria College; Assumption College; Babson College; Berkshire Christian College; Boston College; Boston University; Brandeis University; Bridgewater State College; College of the Holy Cross; Curry College; Eastern Nazarene College; Elms College; Emmanuel College; Fitchburg State College; Framingham State College; Gordon College; Harvard and Radcliffe Colleges; Lesley College; Massachusetts College of Pharmacy & Allied Health Sciences; Mount Holyoke College; Nichols College; North Adams State College; Northeastern University; St. Hyacinth College; Salem State College; Simmons College; Smith College; Southeastern Massachusetts University; Springfield College; Stonehill College; Suffolk University; Tufts University; University of Lowell; Wellesley College; Western New England College; Westfield State College; Wheaton College; Williams College; Worcester Polytechnic Institute; Worcester State College.

MICHIGAN
Adrian College; Albion College; Alma College; Andrews University; Calvin College; Cleary College; Concordia College; Eastern Michigan University; Ferris State College; Grace Bible College; Grand Valley State College; Hillsdale College; Hope College; Kalamazoo College; Lake Superior State College; Lawrence Institute of Technology; Madonna College; Marygrove College; Michigan State University; Northern Michigan University; Northwood Institute; Oakland University; Saginaw Valley State College; St. Mary's College; Siena Heights College; Spring Arbor College; University of Detroit; University of Michigan; University of Michigan/Dearborn; University of Michigan/Flint; Wayne State University; Western Michigan University.

MINNESOTA

Augsburg College; Bemidji State University; Bethel College; Carleton College; College of St. Catherine; College of Saint Teresa; Concordia College/ Moorhead; Concordia College/St. Paul; Gustavus Adolphus College; Hamline University; Mankato State University; St. Olaf College; University of Minnesota/Morris.

MISSISSIPPI

Delta State University; Jackson State University; Mississippi University for Women; University of Mississippi; University of Southern Mississippi; William Carey College.

MISSOURI

Avila College; Central Methodist College; Central Missouri State University; Culver-Stockton College; Drury College; Evangel College; Lindenwood College; Maryville College–St. Louis; Missouri Valley College; Northeast Missouri State University; Northwest Missouri State University; Rockhurst College; Saint Louis University; Southeast Missouri State University; Southwest Baptist University; Southwest Missouri State University; Stephens College; Tarkio College; University of Missouri/Columbia; University of Missouri/ Kansas City; University of Missouri/Rolla; Washington University; Webster University; Westminster College; William Jewel College; William Woods College.

MONTANA

Montana State University; Rocky Mountain College.

NEBRASKA

Chadron State College; College of Saint Mary; Concordia Teachers College; Dana College; Midland Lutheran College; Nebraska Wesleyan University; University of Nebraska/Lincoln; University of Nebraska/Omaha.

NEVADA

University of Nevada/Las Vegas; University of Nevada/Reno.

NEW HAMPSHIRE

Colby-Sawyer College; Dartmouth College; Franklin Pierce College; Hawthorne College; New England College; New Hampshire College; Notre Dame College; Rivier College; St. Anselm's College; University of New Hampshire.

NEW JERSEY

Caldwell College; Drew University; Fairleigh Dickinson University (all campuses); Georgian Court College; Glassboro State University; Jersey City State College; Monmouth College; Montclair State College; Princeton University; Ramapo College of New Jersey; Rutgers University (all campuses); Saint Peter's College; Seton Hall University; Trenton State College; Upsala College; William Paterson College of New Jersey.

NEW YORK

Adelphi University; Albany College of Pharmacy; Barnard College; Canisius College; CUNY/College of Staten Island; CUNY/Lehman College; CUNY/

Hunter College; CUNY/John Jay College; Colgate University; College of New Rochelle; College of Saint Rose; Columbia University; Concordia College; Daemen College; Dowling College; Elmira College; Friends World College; Hartwick College; Hofstra University; Iona College; Ithaca College; King's College; Le Moyne College; Long Island University/C. W. Post; Long Island University/Southampton; Manhattan College; Manhattanville College; Marymount Manhattan College; Mercy College; Molloy College; Mount Saint Mary College; Nazareth College of Rochester; New York Institute of Technology; New York University; Pace University (all campuses); Roberts Wesleyan College; Russell Sage College; St. Bonaventure University; St. Francis College; St. John Fisher College; St. John's University; St. Joseph's College; St. Joseph's College/Suffolk; St. Lawrence University; Siena College; State University of New York (all campuses); Syracuse University; Touro College; University of Rochester; Utica College; Vassar College; Wadhams Hall Seminary-College; Wagner College; Wells College; Yeshiva University.

NORTH CAROLINA
Appalachian State University; Belmont Abbey College; Bennett College; Campbell University; Catawba College; Davidson College; Duke University; East Carolina University; Guilford College; High Point College; Lenoir-Rhyne College; Mars Hill College; Methodist College; North Carolina State University; Pfeiffer College; Queens College; Sacred Heart College; St. Andrews Presbyterian College; Salem College; University of North Carolina/Asheville; University of North Carolina/Wilmington; Wake Forest University; Western Carolina University; Wingate College.

NORTH DAKOTA
Jamestown College; Mary College; North Dakota State University; University of North Dakota.

OHIO
Antioch College; Ashland College; Baldwin-Wallace College; Bluffton College; Borromeo College of Ohio; Bowling Green State University; Case Western Reserve; Cleveland State University; College of Mount St. Joseph on the Ohio; Defiance College; Denison University; Dyke College; Hiram College; John Carroll University; Lake Erie College; Malone College; Marietta College; Miami University; Mount Vernon Nazarene College; Muskingum College; Notre Dame College of Ohio; Ohio Dominican College; Ohio State University (all campuses); Ohio University; Ohio Wesleyan University; Otterbein College; University of Cincinnati; University of Steubenville; University of Toledo; Walsh College; Wilberforce University; Wilmington College; Wittenberg University; Wright State University; Xavier University.

OKLAHOMA
Oklahoma Baptist University; Oklahoma City University; Oklahoma State University; Phillips University; University of Oklahoma; University of Tulsa.

OREGON
Eastern Oregon State College; George Fox College; Lewis and Clark College; Oregon State University; Portland State University; Southern Oregon State

College; University of Oregon; University of Portland; Warner Pacific College; Western Baptist College; Western Oregon State College; Willamette University.

PENNSYLVANIA

Allegheny College; Allentown College of St. Francis de Sales; Alliance College; Beaver College; Bloomsburg University of Pennsylvania; Bryn Mawr College; Bucknell University; Cabrini College; California University of Pennsylvania; Carnegie-Mellon University; Cedar Crest College; Chatham College; Chestnut Hill College; Cheyney University of Pennsylvania; Clarion University of Pennsylvania; Drexel University; Duquesne University; Eastern College; Edinboro University of Pennsylvania; Elizabethtown College; Franklin and Marshall College; Gannon University; Geneva College; Gettysburg College; Grove City College; Gwynedd-Mercy College; Holy Family College; Immaculata College; King's College; La Salle University; Lafayette College; Lebanon Valley College; Lincoln University; Lycoming College; Marywood College; Mercyhurst College; Messiah College; Moravian College; Muhlenberg College; Neumann College; Philadelphia College of Textiles and Science; Point Park College; Robert Morris College; Saint Joseph's University; Saint Vincent College; Seton Hill College; Slippery Rock University of Pennsylvania; Susquehanna University; Swarthmore College; Temple University; Thiel College; University of Pennsylvania; University of Pittsburgh; University of Philadelphia (all campuses); University of Scranton; Ursinus College; Valley Forge Christian College; Villa Maria College; Washington and Jefferson College; Waynesburg College; West Chester University of Pennsylvania; Westminster College; Widener University; Wilkes College; York College of Pennsylvania.

RHODE ISLAND

Brown University; Bryant College; Providence College; Rhode Island College; Salve-Regina/Newport College; University of Rhode Island.

SOUTH CAROLINA

Central Wesleyan College; Clemson University; Coker College; College of Charleston; Converse College; Erskine College; Francis Marion College; Furman University; Lander College; Limestone College; Newberry College; Presbyterian College; South Carolina State College; University of South Carolina; University of South Carolina/Spartanburg; University of South Carolina, Coastal Carolina College; Winthrop College; Wofford College.

SOUTH DAKOTA

Augustana College; Black Hills State College; Sioux Falls College; South Dakota State University.

TENNESSEE

Austin Peay State University; Bethel College; Christian Brothers College; David Lipscomb College; East Tennessee State University; Freed-Hardeman College; King College; Lambuth College; Lee College; Lincoln Memorial University; Maryville College; Memphis College of Art; Middle Tennessee State

University; Milligan College; Rhodes College; Tennessee Technological University; Tennessee Temple University; Trevecca Nazarene College; Union University; University of Tennessee at Chattanooga; University of Tennessee/Knoxville; Vanderbilt University.

TEXAS

Abilene Christian University; Angelo State University; Baylor University; Bishop College; East Texas Baptist University; East Texas State University; Hardin-Simmons University; Jarvis Christian College; Lamar University; LeTourneau College; Lubbock Christian College; McMurry College; Midwestern State University; North Texas State University; Prairie View A&M University; Rice University; St. Edward's University; St. Mary's University of San Antonio; Schreiner College; Southern Methodist University; Southwestern University; Southwest Texas State University; Stephen F. Austin State University; Texas A&M University; Texas A&M University/Galveston; Texas Christian University; Texas Lutheran College; Texas Tech University; Texas Wesleyan College; Trinity College; University of Dallas; University of St. Thomas; University of Texas/Arlington; University of Texas/Austin; University of Texas/El Paso; West Texas State University.

UTAH

Brigham Young University; University of Utah; Utah State University; Weber State College; Westminster College.

VERMONT

Castleton State College; Lyndon State College; Marlboro College; Middlebury College; Norwich University; Saint Michael's College; Trinity College; University of Vermont; Vermont College of Norwich University.

VIRGINIA

Averett College; Bridgewater College; Christopher Newport College; College of William and Mary; Emory and Henry College; George Mason University; Hampden-Sydney College; James Madison University; Liberty University; Longwood College; Lynchburg College; Mary Baldwin College; Marymount University; Norfolk State University; Old Dominion University; Radford University; Randolph-Macon College; Randolph-Macon Women's College; Roanoke College; Sweet Briar College; University of Richmond; Virginia Commonwealth University; Virginia Polytechnic Institute and State University; Virginia Wesleyan College; Washington and Lee University.

WASHINGTON

Central Washington University; Eastern Washington University; Evergreen State College; Gonzaga University; Northwest College; Pacific Lutheran College; Saint Martin's College; Seattle Pacific University; Seattle University; University of Puget Sound; University of Washington; Washington State University; Western Washington University; Whitman College; Whitworth College.

WEST VIRGINIA

Alderson-Broaddus College; Concord College; Fairmont State College; Shepherd College; University of Charleston; West Virginia Institute of Technology; West Virginia State College; West Virginia University; West Virginia Wesleyan College.

WISCONSIN

Beloit College; Cardinal Stritch College; Carthage College; Edgewood College; Lakeland College; Lawrence University; Marian College of Fond du Lac; Mount Mary College; Mount Senario College; Northland College; St. Norbert College; University of Wisconsin/Green Bay; University of Wisconsin/Madison; University of Wisconsin/Milwaukee; University of Wisconsin/Parkside; University of Wisconsin/Stevens Point; University of Wisconsin/Whitewater.

WYOMING

University of Wyoming.

PUERTO RICO

Catholic University of Puerto Rico; University of the Sacred Heart.

9

EARN WHILE YOU LEARN

More than half of today's undergraduates hold part-time jobs during their academic year. For most the salaries they receive represent the bulk of their contribution to their own education. Without this added income many students couldn't afford to remain in college.

"Working my way through college" is now such a normal part of a student's life that the concept is supported by several formal programs that can help make the experience financially rewarding and intellectually enriching.

In this chapter we'll look at four such programs: the College Work-Study Program, co-operative education, federal co-op programs, and the Federal Junior Fellowship Program. Each of these has its own distinct format. Each can make its own contribution to your overall education experience and help cut your college costs. Then we'll look at how an internship can help you save money and advance your future career.

The College Work-Study Program. A federally sponsored campus-based program, College Work-Study (CWS) is designed for students with demonstrated financial need. Participants must be enrolled for at least half-time study. It is open to both undergraduate and graduate students. Most CWS jobs are located on campus, although they can also be at nearby nonprofit organizations such as hospitals and charitable organizations.

The typical CWS student works on-campus for 10 to 15 hours each week, although it is possible to work as much as 40 hours a week. The salary is generally the minimum wage. Program guidelines ask that college officials administering the program attempt to find jobs that have some relation to the student's course of study. While this happens occasionally, the on-campus jobs usually tend to be unrelated to studies, such as grounds keeper, library aide, cafeteria worker, office clerk, and faculty aide.

To participate in CWS you must meet the following eligibility requirements:

- You must be a student at an approved two- or four-year college or university.
- You must prove financial need through your student financial aid application.
- You must be a citizen or permanent resident of the United States, or prove your intent to become a permanent resident.
- You must have a high school diploma or equivalent.
- You must make satisfactory academic progress as determined by your college.
- You must not owe on federal or state grants you've received while attending the college at which you're enrolled.

The CWS Program does have some limitations, especially if you are attending college in an area where off-campus part-time jobs are plentiful and the salaries higher than minimum wage, but it does have its rewards, especially if the college can place you in a job related to your major. If you are fortunate enough to obtain a position in your field, be sure to get a letter of recommendation from your superior before leaving the job. This may help when you enter the job market.

You can apply for a CWS job through the college's financial aid office. The financial aid administrator determines who gets placed in which available jobs. Since the money to finance these jobs is granted by the federal government, there are guidelines the administrator must follow when selecting students for participation.

These include your financial need, what other aid you may be receiving, your needs in comparison to other applicants for CWS positions, and your ability to maintain acceptable academic standards. A CWS award is given for a specific amount, say $1,200. When you've earned the $1,200, you must resign the position. Since funds received through the CWS program are more desirable than a loan that has to be repaid, do everything possible to participate. A good approach is to write a letter to the financial aid administrator explaining your willingness to work to earn money for your education. The letter becomes a part of your file in the financial aid office and is readily available when your financial aid package is prepared.

To locate colleges that participate in the CWS Program see the Appendix, *College Profiles for Cost Cutters*.

Co-operative Education. Co-operative education is an exciting alternative to traditional classroom study that differs markedly from a jobs program like CWS. It's exciting because co-op education offers a myriad of educational, financial, and career opportunities.

The typical co-op student is given a responsible position in his or her field of interest and study. The company providing the job understands the student is there to learn as well as perform, so most co-op employers, in agreement with the college, make an extra effort to create the right kind of environment for the co-op worker.

The national average annual earnings for co-op students is $7,000, which more than covers most costs at many colleges. Generally, the money earned through co-op jobs is figured in with the student's financial aid package, effectively reducing the student's need for borrowed money. An added feature of co-op education is that many employers consider their co-op student/workers full-time employees, making them eligible for regular employee benefits.

———

As a math major at Wichita State University, Molly Maxton wasn't sure what her career goals were. After taking a co-op position as an air-traffic controller trainee at the control tower in Wichita's airport, she found the career she had been searching for. An added feature of her experience was the $248 weekly salary that financed her entire education.

———

Besides providing a student with employment in his or her field of study, co-op jobs are usually designed to give the student assignments that are progressively more challenging and informative.

The first co-operative education program began in 1906 at the University of Cincinnati. It was the brainchild of Herman Schneider, dean of the school of engineering. Schneider hoped to accomplish two goals through his program. One was to provide meaningful employment to his engineering students who needed to work during their college years. Most were engaged in menial jobs unrelated to their engineering studies and career goals. Schneider also believed there were aspects of most professions that were better taught with hands-on experience in the field instead of in the classroom.

Dean Schneider's first program for his engineering students alternated classroom participation with meaningful employment in engineering-related jobs with companies in the Cincinnati area. He split his students into two groups. Each group spent one week in class and one week at the selected job. While one group worked, the other studied.

Three years later Northeastern University, then known as the Polytechnic School of the YMCA Evening Institute, began its own co-operative education program for engineering students modeled after Schneider's program. By the end of 1919 ten institutes of higher learning were providing co-operative education opportunities to their engineering students. Among these were the Massachusetts Institute of Technology, Drexel and Marquette universities, and the Rochester Institute of Technology.

The same year the University of Cincinnati expanded its program to students in the school of business. Two years later Antioch College initiated the first co-op program for liberal arts students. During the 1920s and 1930s the idea of integrating college study with the experiences of the real workaday world spread to colleges and universities throughout the country.

At the start of the 1960s, sixty-one four-year colleges and universities and ten two-year colleges were offering their students the opportunity to participate in co-operative education programs.

Today, over 900 colleges and universities, both four- and two-year schools, have active co-operative education programs. Co-op is available in almost every curriculum, with some 200,000 students participating. About 50,000 employers hire co-op students. Although some are large corporations, most are small companies and organizations that hire one to three students at a time.

———

Lance Goodman participated in co-operative education while he was majoring in aerospace mechanical engineering at the University of Central Florida. His first co-op job was at the Kennedy Space Center as a member of a crew building equipment for use on the Spacelab. During one year his earnings were $7,200, which more than covered his expenses of $4,700, including tuition, books, entertainment, and the monthly payments on his car. In addition, Goodman's work experience contributed immeasurably to his learning experience at the university.

———

Co-operative education students often find their work assignments are not only related to their college studies and career goals but are also interesting and challenging. Russell J. Rowlett, math professor at the University of Tennessee, has said his co-op students were "placed in charge of production lines; wrote programs to analyze on-line data from spacecraft; had personal responsibility for customer accounts; coauthored published research; designed and programmed systems to be used daily by hundreds of other employees."

Co-op students have worked as library assistant in the Library of Congress; copyperson in the editorial department of *The New York Times;* shuttle resources assistant for NASA; physical therapy aide at Denver General Hospital; assistant to the general director of the Banque Franco-Portugaise in Paris; accounting assistant at Arthur Anderson & Company; traffic analyst for Continental Forest Industries; programmer for the Armagh Observatory in Northern Ireland; industrial engineering analyst for Tektronix; nursing assistant at Johns Hopkins Hospital; and pharmacy intern at Massachusetts General. With over 200,000 college students participating in co-op programs, the list of positions they hold would fill an entire volume. The few mentioned here give an idea of the level of the positions available through co-operative education programs.

Co-operative education is open to all college students, providing the college you attend has a program. This is not a need-based program. Usually the only requirement of most colleges is that the participating student maintain minimum academic standards, generally a grade-point average of 2.5 on a 4.0 scale. There are no age requirements for participation, and the programs are open to both traditional and nontraditional students.

Co-operative education is part career builder and part cost cutter. The benefits you can derive from participation in a co-op program can far outweigh some of the social activity you may have to forgo, although it is possible to arrange a position close enough to the campus so you can continue participation in social and extracurricular campus activities. It's even possible to arrange your work schedule so that you remain on campus, for example, during the season of your sport if you participate in intercollegiate athletics.

Let's look at some of the benefits you'll receive as a co-operative education student.

1. You'll be paid a salary commensurate with the work you'll be doing. With the average co-op student earning over $7,000 before taxes, your earnings can go a long way toward paying for your education.
2. Because you'll be working in the field of your career interest, you'll have an opportunity to evaluate that field before the traditional student who must wait until graduation to find the job he or she wants. This may help you decide if you have made the right career choice. If you find the field isn't what you expected, or doesn't have the opportunities you seek, you still have time to

change the direction of your education and the field in which your next co-op assignment will be. Studies have shown that co-op students have a clearer and more specific sense of their career goals than traditional college students.

3. Your co-op jobs allow you to put what you have learned in the classroom to the test in the "real world." Many students have found the experience gives meaning to what they are studying because the theories learned in the class are reinforced when applied in the work environment. The result of seeing learning in action creates a more motivated student.

4. The real work experience and the relationships you can establish while on co-op assignments can contribute toward greatly improved job prospects after graduation. About 80 percent of co-operative education students receive a job offer for a permanent position from a co-op participating employer; 63 percent get a job offer from their final co-op employer. Companies that participate in co-operative education programs like the opportunity it gives them to evaluate students before they actually become permanent employees. Not only does it take the gamble out of hiring someone fresh out of college, but they know that co-op students are better equipped to make career decisions than most students and tend to stay with the company longer and ultimately gain more responsibility than traditional students. The attitude of many co-op employers is summed up in a statement by Walter Mattson of The New York Times Company: "The co-op program is a pipeline. Entering at one end are motivated students. Emerging at the other are mature adults who become innovative, well-rounded employees and citizens."

5. If you decide not to accept employment from a company you've worked for through a co-op assignment, the experience, your participation in the program, and the letters of recommendation you request may help you land a position with the company of your choice.

6. Working alongside others improves your abilities to relate and to work as part of a team. Although some teachers attempt to improve their student's interpersonal relationships, they can only do so through artificially devised groupings. In the work environment you are required to realistically consider the feelings, ideas, and responsibilities of others if you are going to accomplish your assignment. Developing these skills while still in college helps prevent the "culture shock" many college graduates experience when they leave academia for the real world.

7. As a college graduate with co-operative education experience in your chosen field you may command a higher starting salary than nonco-op students and may also receive promotions and merit increases more frequently. Studies conducted by Arthur D. Little, Inc., and the Detroit Institute of Technology substantiate the improved career growth of co-op graduates over traditional college graduates. Three succeeding presidents of General Motors—Elliott Estes, Edward Cole, and F. James McDonald—participated in co-operative education programs.

Kim Allen Chamberlin graduated from the University of Cincinnati in 1982, after taking part in the university's co-op program for architecture students. During his college career he held co-op assignments of increasing responsibility with four different companies. Chamberlin believes his co-op experience resulted in his career being at least two years ahead of where it would have been if he hadn't the work experience co-op provided him.

Each college designs its own program, so they vary from one college to another. While most colleges offer co-op to their students as an option, others, like Drexel University, treat it as a mandatory part of their undergraduate curriculum.

Most programs at four-year colleges require that freshmen remain on campus during their first year, permitting co-op participation to start during the student's sophomore year.

Four-year colleges use either a parallel schedule or an alternating schedule in their co-op programs. The parallel schedule has students attend classes in the morning and work at their jobs in the afternoon, or vice versa. Under the alternating schedule, which is the most commonly used, students attend classes full time for a prescribed period, which might be a semester or quarter, then work at their co-op assignment for a similar period. This rotation continues usually until the student accumulates the equivalent of one year's work experience. Classroom time lost during the work assignments is generally recovered in summer sessions. Some colleges award credits toward your degree for your work experience on co-op assignments.

A small number of colleges require students in selected co-op programs such as engineering and science to remain in the program for five years before graduation, instead of the usual four. These programs are in the minority, but even if you do choose a five-year program, this is one instance where the time spent is not necessarily money spent since your salary will probably more than cover your expenses. Two-year community and junior colleges usually use the parallel schedule for co-op programs, where the students' day is divided between classroom study and their work assignment.

Over one-quarter of the students currently participating in co-operative education programs are business majors, while a slightly smaller number are engineering students. The remaining students come from virtually every other major, including liberal arts.

———

Cindy Carr was still in high school when she decided she wanted a career in food-processing management. While attending Oregon State University's Food Science and Technology Department Cindy signed up for the university's co-op program on an alternating schedule. As a quality-control supervisor at the nearby Birdseye plant she supervised 20 people, and earned $7,200 her first term there.

———

Co-operative education programs do not guarantee you'll get the job you want. Usually you must be interviewed by the prospective employer before you are hired for the assignment. The assistance you receive from the college during this and the work phase of your co-op assignment varies from school to school. An important consideration for any student who wants to participate in a co-op program while attending college is the support you will receive from the administrators of the program. A well-run professional program provides a counselor who can help you through your preparation for the job interview and be available during your entire career as a co-op student.

If the financial and experiential benefits of co-operative education are important to you, then your selection of a college must include an examination of the college's approach to co-op education. To help with your selection process, the Appendix, *College Profiles for Cost Cutters,* shows you which colleges offer co-op programs.

The next place to look is the college's catalogue. Is co-operative education discussed? If so, is it available to students in your major? Some colleges offer co-op only in specific majors, while others offer it to all students. Does the description sound as if the college has made a commitment to the program, or is it just something that's available if you really want it?

Since it's foolish to enroll in a college without first visiting it, let's assume that you're going to spend a short time on campus before making your decision. Before you do, call the office responsible for administering the co-operative education program. Make an appointment to meet a counselor. Once you're there get a feel for what goes on. Does the look of the office and staff give you confidence that it is an ongoing part of the college's life? Ask about the department's budget. Is it substantial enough to support the number of students it claims are in the program? A half-hearted commitment by the college might mean a corresponding half-hearted effort to locate employers to participate in the program, resulting in a limited number of available positions. Ask how many students are currently working at co-op job assignments in your field. Ask who the employers are. This kind of information can give you a feel for the strength and soundness of the program. Does the school publish a handbook for co-operative education students? This is usually a sign that the program has been around some time and will continue to exist during your college career.

Ask to see current job descriptions of co-op students in your major. Do they sound like the kind of assignments you'd like? Do the jobs sound as if they provide progressive responsibility with consecutive assignments? Find out how much they pay. Ask what the staff is doing to get more employers involved in the program. Find out the ratio between students seeking assignments and those receiving them.

Ask to speak to some co-op students. Find out how they feel about the program. Are they getting the assignments they feel will help them, or do the jobs fall short of expectations? Do they have constant contact with the co-op counselors while on their assignments, or are they left on their own? Do the counselors work closely with the students in locating jobs, helping them get the best ones, and resolving problems that may arise on the job?

Don't be afraid to ask all the questions you feel are important to you. If the co-operative education staff is professional in their approach to their responsibilities, they'll be glad to share that information with you. They'll be impressed by the obvious value your questions put on their co-op program. After all, that's how these people make their living. Contented students are usually eager to share their experiences, so don't hesitate to dig deep into the college's co-operative education program before you enroll.

Federal Co-operative Education Program. The largest employer of co-operative education students is the federal government. As with anything associated with the federal government, the figures are staggering. Government agencies employ some 15,000 co-op students at almost 2,000 work sites throughout the country. Federal agencies have co-op agreements with almost 800 colleges and universities, and accept students seeking associate, bachelor's, and graduate degrees.

Nearly every kind of government facility, from a naval base to the local Social Security office or Veterans Administration hospital, is a site for co-operative education work assignments.

The variety of co-op job assignments available at federal agencies is almost unlimited. The salaries are based on the civil service schedule, so a student just starting out on a co-op assignment can generally expect to start as a GS-2, for which the current pay is $5.20 per hour.

Because of the size of many of the agencies involved and their experience working with co-op students, colleges are given unusual flexibility in scheduling co-op assignments. Besides the alternate and parallel schedules discussed in the previous section, there is a summer schedule for students working only during summer vacations. This is the least common plan, but it is available for those students who want to make use of it.

To learn which colleges and universities participate in federal co-op programs, see the Appendix, *College Profiles for Cost Cutters.*

Federal Junior Fellowship Program. This federal program is substantially different from the co-op program. The two should not be confused. Because it is so decentralized, the Federal Junior Fellowship Program is one of the least-known programs of its kind. Participation is limited to 5,000 students at any one time, but because it is so unknown there were over 3,000 vacancies during a recent year.

The program is open to high school seniors who meet the following eligibility requirements:

- You must be in the upper 10 percent of your graduating class.
- You must be accepted for full-time enrollment as a bachelor's candidate at an accredited college.
- You must demonstrate you need the earnings to meet college expenses based on financial need and family income.
- You must be a citizen at the time of appointment.
- You must express an interest in pursuing a career with the federal government after graduation.

A Junior Fellow begins working for a federal agency after graduation, not while he or she is still in high school. The work can be performed during any extended break in class schedule, such as summer vacation, and Christmas and spring breaks. The first assignment starts the summer right after high school graduation.

As with the co-op program, the salary you receive is based on the civil service schedule. During the first year you are a GS-2, which currently pays $5.20 per hour; the second year you are eligible to be promoted to a GS-3, which now pays $5.67 per hour; and so on up to a GS-5.

While you participate in the program you are required to perform your work satisfactorily, maintain minimum academic standards, continue in the major you originally selected, and remain with the same federal agency throughout the extent of your participation. An important point to remember is that you must be sure of both your major and the agency you work at if you want to reap the benefits from this program. You can't go back and reselect as you can in the co-op program. Another big difference is that your college doesn't have to be connected to this program in any way. You can attend the college of your choice without worrying about it having an agreement with the federal agency at which you work. The only requirement is the college be accredited by one of the recognized accrediting agencies.

Since positions are filled by students whose college major relates to the position available, it may be difficult to find the right job. Based on experience, almost 80 percent of the Junior Fellow positions are filled by students majoring in one of the following areas:

Accounting

Biological Sciences

Business Administration

Computer Science

Engineering

Mathematics

Physical Sciences

The remaining jobs generally require majors in library science, psychology, sociology, political science, history, education, and other liberal arts fields. Few positions are ever available for students majoring in art, music, or drama.

This is an excellent program for high school seniors who meet the requirements. Besides the on-the-job experience and connections it provides, the salary is attractive and you are still able to supplement your income with a part-time job elsewhere during evenings and weekends while school is in session.

After graduation, the agency you have been working for as Junior Fellow may offer you a full-time permanent position. If you receive such an offer, you are free to accept or reject it.

While most Junior Fellows are hired as permanent employees at the GS-5 salary grade, those in occupations where there are more vacancies than applicants may be eligible to start at the much higher GS-7 level.

The biggest reason this program remains a mystery to many high school counselors is the way in which recruitment is done. Since there is no central authority for the program, each agency at each location that expects to have Junior Fellow positions available is responsible for filling them. The normal procedure is to send notifications of the positions available, along with applications, to high schools in the area in the early spring. Each school is expected to designate a Junior Fellow coordinator (usually a guidance counselor) who is supposed to inform the senior class about the openings. Candidates for the positions are nominated by the school from among the students who meet the qualifications and express an interest in one or more of the openings.

Somewhere in this loose communications chain much of the information seems to be getting lost. If you are a high school senior and expect to meet the entrance requirements for the program, contact your guidance counselor. If he or she isn't knowledgeable about the Federal Junior Fellowship Program, bring this book along with you. If by early spring the school hasn't received information about Junior Fellowship openings at nearby federal facilities, your counselor should immediately begin calling federal agency personnel directors to ask if openings are available.

Internships. Another alternative available to college students is to find an internship. While not as financially attractive as co-op or Junior Fellowship assignments (many internships pay little or no salary), they still provide the other benefits of the more formal programs. This is especially true for liberal arts majors, for whom co-op jobs are always scarce.

Each semester over 1.5 million college students take part in internships. Some last for a single semester or summer vacation, while others are of longer duration.

An internship is a learning experience where the student works in the field of his or her choice, similar to an apprentice learning a trade. In many cases your work schedule may be adjusted around your academic schedule. You might work evenings, weekends, during scheduled breaks, such as summer and Christmas, or one day each week. Virtually every internship is different.

If an internship interests you, your first step is to find out if your college has an active internship program. Ask your academic department head or contact the college's placement or career planning office. Sometimes colleges award academic credit to students who participate in internships related to their major. Some employers may kick in a small stipend if you appear to be a good prospect for an intern. Since most internships are not part of formal programs, you are usually free to get out of an internship whatever you can negotiate. When you find one you like, try for that credit and a small salary to "cover expenses."

If your college has no program for locating internships, it's up to you to find one. The college library should have a directory of available internships on hand. If you can't find one there, you can order the National Directory of Internships, for $16, from the National Society for Internships and Experiential Education, 3509 Haworth Drive, Suite 207, Raleigh, NC 27609. While the price is a bit hefty, the directory does list over 26,000 internships across the country, including some that pay a salary and some that help you get college credit for your participation. The organizations offering internships are indexed by geographic location, subject area, and by name. Each entry contains everything you need to know, including the number of internships available, if a stipend or salary is included, the type of work interns do, the duration and timing of the internships, if the employer will help you get credit, and much more.

While an internship can help reduce your college costs through either a salary or the awarding of credit, its primary purpose is to expose you to the real world of work in your field of interest. It's up to you to make the most of an internship both by what you can learn, and the connections you can make with people who might later be able to help you land a job in your field.

If you want to seriously consider an internship as part of your college experience, I recommend another book sponsored by the National Society for Internships and Experiential Education. It is *The Experienced Hand: A Student Manual for Making the Most of an*

Internship. It includes advice on locating and evaluating an internship, how to get faculty support for academic credit for your internship, and how to apply for and win the internship you want. The book sells for $6.95 and can be ordered from Carroll Press, P.O. Box 8113, Cranston, RI 02920.

10

HOW TO GET UNCLE SAM TO PAY

If you don't have money for college, or enough money to see you through the entire four years, getting help from the United States armed forces is an option to consider. The armed services offers financial assistance to qualifying college students.

Before you start protesting that you don't want to spend the rest of your life in a military uniform in exchange for the armed services paying for your college education, understand one important fact: for the most part the military expects surprisingly little from you in return for paying your education bill. Sure, you have to make a commitment to spend some time in the military, but keep in mind that no one is going to pay for your college education without the expectation of receiving something in return. And you never know—you might discover that life in one of the military services, especially as a commissioned officer, is more attractive than you originally thought.

Each year the United States military spends about $1 billion on college education programs. Unlike other financial assistance programs that are based on the student's needs, the distribution of this money is based on criteria such as the student's commitment to serve in the military after graduation, the student's current participation in active duty or previous active duty, and the student's performance as a scholar and well-rounded citizen.

Even if you never considered becoming a member of the armed forces, read this chapter thoroughly and with an open mind. The opportunities offered by military assistance programs are impressive, while the payback is slight in comparison to the longterm benefits you receive.

This chapter deals with military-sponsored programs for college students. There are other educational programs operated by the armed services, such as the service academies, a multitude of educational opportunities for men and women on active duty, and educational benefits for veterans.

One final point: It is possible that although you never considered joining the military, you may find a program in this chapter that sounds exactly right for you. If this happens, it's important that you examine your attitude toward the military and your participation in it. If you have a completely negative attitude about the armed services, then you might be making a grave mistake attempting to enroll in a military-connected program. These programs lead to a commission in the military as an officer. How do you feel about the possibility of becoming a military officer? Does that kind of responsibility sound like more than you want in life? If you have a religious or other objection to taking up arms even to defend the Constitution of the United States, then it's obvious these programs are not for you.

Besides serving your country, being an officer in the armed services is a good way to develop your management and leadership skills. Many employers recognize this and look favorably toward an applicant with several years as a military officer on his or her resume.

The most popular military-sponsored program for college students is the Reserve Officers' Training Corps, or ROTC. The Army, Navy, and Air Force each have ROTC programs. Students desiring to become Marine Corps officers participate in the Naval ROTC.

Over 15,000 military officers are commissioned through ROTC programs each year. There are two basic types of ROTC programs offered by all three military services. The first is a scholarship program in which all or nearly all of your college expenses are paid by the military. The second is a nonscholarship program in which you participate in ROTC training and receive only a monthly allowance. Since the thrust of this book is cutting college costs we will examine only the scholarship-based programs.

A college or university participates in ROTC by becoming either a "host" or "cross-enrollment" institution. Host colleges have active ROTC units on campus, while the cross-enrollment colleges have agreements with host institutions that permit their students to take part in the host ROTC program. The Army has over 300 host colleges and universities and more than 1,000 colleges engaged in cross-enrollment. The Navy has 65 host colleges and over 115 cross-enrollment institutions. The Air Force has 151 hosts and over 650 cross-enrollment colleges. So, as you can see, there are many colleges and universities to choose from if you decide ROTC is for you.

Within the ROTC scholarship program there are several alternatives, based on the number of years you participate. While most scholarship students take part in the four-year programs, some sign on for three or even two years. Each of these options is discussed in the breakdown of each service's program.

When you become a member of the ROTC you're known as either a cadet (Army and Air Force) or midshipman (Navy). Besides taking courses required by your subject major you take military-science courses as a part of your electives, participate in drills and training with your ROTC unit, and attend summer training camps. When you graduate you join the armed service as either a regular or reserve officer, depending on the program you have selected.

In return for your commitment to a predetermined time of active or reserve duty, the military provides you a scholarship that pays your college tuition, costs of textbooks, and instructional fees. You also receive a tax-free allowance of $100 per month while school is in session, and you are paid a regular salary for participation in summer training.

As a part-time cadet or midshipman you are required to wear your uniform, which is supplied free, only when you attend an ROTC class or drill. In all other aspects your college life is similar to that of any other student who is paying his or her own way or running up huge debts for the same education.

ROTC scholarships are awarded annually. The awards are based on a competitive selection process in which consideration is given to your high school class standing, your SAT and ACT scores, and your participation in extracurricular activities and demonstrated leadership qualities in those activities. Remember, while you may be looking for a free or low-cost quality education, the military is looking for its future officers and leaders.

While each of the three services operates its ROTC slightly differently from the others, the basic benefits to participating college students are the same. The benefits you'll receive as an ROTC cadet or midshipman are:

- Tuition and academic fees
- Books
- A tax-free monthly allowance for the school year of $100
- Free uniforms

- Salary for summer training of approximately $400 monthly
- A travel allowance from your home to the college at the start of your freshman year
- Free flights on military passenger aircraft on a space-available basis

What's this package worth? Just the strictly educational aspects of it could be worth as much as $50,000, depending on the college you choose.

Sounds attractive, doesn't it? Obviously it is, since so many high school seniors apply each year that less than 20 percent of applicants for ROTC four-year scholarships are accepted into the Army, Navy, and Air Force programs.

The time to prepare for applying for an ROTC scholarship is during your sophomore or junior year in high school. You need to maintain high grades, and generally be in at least the top 25 percent of your class. You should participate in as many extracurricular activities as possible. Try to become a leader in those activities.

During the 1986–87 school year 96 percent of the students awarded four-year scholarships by the Army ranked in the top 25 percent of their class, while 12 percent ranked first; 74 percent had been class president or other class officer; 71 percent were National Honor Society members; and 76 percent were varsity letter winners. As you can see, ROTC is not a program for slouches. Besides paying for your college education the ROTC can be a truly rewarding experience, but it is difficult to get into and demanding while you participate.

Now let's take a closer look at the individual programs offered by each of the armed services.

The Naval Reserve Officers Training Corps. High school seniors interested in becoming either Navy or Marine Corps officers should seek a scholarship from the NROTC. For those selecting the Marine Corps option the training is the same as for Navy candidates for the first two years. Military science classes during their junior and senior years are based on subjects relevant to the Marine Corps. Marine Corps option midshipmen take their final summer training at Quantico, Virginia.

General Eligibility Requirements

1. You must be a citizen of the United States.
2. You must be 17 years old by September 1 of the year you start college and less than 21 on June 30 of that year.

3. You must have a high school diploma or equivalency certificate by the end of August of the year you enter the NROTC.
4. You must meet the Navy's physical standards.
5. You must be accepted by a college or university with an NROTC unit on campus or a cross-enrollment agreement with one.
6. You must plan to pursue a course of study leading to a bachelor's degree in almost any field other than a health profession.
7. To qualify for the Navy portion of the program you must attain a score of at least 430 verbal and 520 math on the SAT, or at least 18 in English and 24 in math on the ACT. For the Marine Corps option you need a minimum of 1,000 combined math and verbal on the SAT or 45 combined math and English on the ACT.

Academic Requirements

1. You must complete all requirements for a bachelor's degree in accordance with the college or university's rules.
2. You are expected to maintain above-average grades.
3. Future Navy officers must take one year of calculus and one year of calculus-based physics; future Marine officers are required to take courses in national affairs and security policy.
4. Regardless of your academic major, you are required to take the following naval science courses, for which the college will grant you credit. The amount of credit depends on the college.
   Introduction to Naval Science
   Naval Ships Systems I (engineering)
   Naval Ships Systems II (weapons)
   Seapower and Maritime Affairs
   Navigation and Naval Operations I and II (for Navy)
   Leadership and Management I and II (for Navy)
   Evolution of Warfare (for Marine Corps)
   Amphibious Warfare (for Marine Corps)
5. You must take part in three summer training periods of about four to six weeks each. They may take place on board ship or at a shore base.

If you are selected as a finalist in the competition, you will be required to complete an application that includes your high school transcript, teacher recommendations, and a report on your extracurricular activities. You will then be interviewed by a panel of Navy or Marine Corps officers and take a medical examination.

Military Service Requirements. After graduation as a Navy midshipman you will be expected to:

1. Accept a commission in either the Navy or the Marine Corps, if offered.
2. Serve a minimum of four years on active duty with the Navy or Marine Corps and four years on inactive duty.

For additional information, including an applicant questionnaire and a list of affiliated colleges, as well as a schedule of closing dates for the coming year, either visit the NROTC unit on a campus near you, or write:

> NROTC Scholarship Program
> Post Office Box 3060
> Hyattsville, MD 20784

Other Navy and Marine Corps Programs

Two-Year Scholarships. The Navy also has a two-year ROTC program with many of the same benefits as the four-year program outlined above. It is open to college students completing their sophomore year in a four-year college or to those transferring from a two-year college. Only a small number of two-year scholarships are generally available. Students accepted are required to spend six weeks at the Naval Science Institute at Newport, Rhode Island, during the summer before their junior year. This time is spent bringing them up to date with the training they missed the first two years. Students are reimbursed for transportation to and from Newport and are paid for the six weeks they spend there.

Nonscholarship NROTC. The Navy offers both four- and two-year nonscholarship ROTC programs that are similar to the scholarship programs, except they don't pay for your tuition or for books other than those used for naval science classes. In addition, the $100 monthly tax-free allowance is available only during the student's junior and senior years. The active duty requirement for nonscholarship participants is three years.

Marine Corps Platoon Leaders Class. This is a program with many rewards, but it is definitely designed for only a few. It is about as tough as the stereotypical Marine Corps drill instructor. It's open to college freshmen, sophomores, and juniors. There is no active involvement while you are attending school, other than eligibility to receive an allowance of $100 for each month of the academic year. All training takes place during the summer months at Officer Candidate School at Quantico, Virginia. There are two summer training sessions of six weeks each or one of ten weeks for juniors. You are paid for all transportation, supplied meals and books, and receive a salary. You must maintain a 2.0 grade-point average (GPA), but be aware that the current qualifying GPA is 2.7.

This program offers a unique opportunity for those who don't qualify for an NROTC scholarship but want to become Marine Corps officers. Besides the financial assistance it provides, the time you spend in the program while in college counts toward your pay when you are commissioned after graduation. This means you start your military service with three years' seniority over second lieutenants who came through ROTC, and you receive thousands of dollars more in pay.

That this program is tough is borne out by the following statistics: 25 to 30 percent of the participants don't make it through the first summer training session; another 10 to 15 percent drop out before they have to return for the second session; and still another 10 to 15 percent fail to complete the second summer session. Less than 50 percent of participants in this program ever reach their commission, and these were people who passed the rigorous physical requirements.

In describing this program one Marine officer told me to think of the worst stories I had heard about Parris Island, and then multiply them by five to equal the rigor of the training in this program. For more information about the Platoon Leaders Class contact:

> Marine Corps Opportunities
> Box 38901
> Los Angeles, CA 90038-9986

Nuclear Propulsion Officer Candidate Program. This program was designed to help the Navy attract officer candidates with strong engineering, physics, chemistry, or math majors. You must have a high grade-point average to qualify for this highly selective program. Once selected you receive a $3,000 enlistment bonus and are paid a minimum of $1,000 each month until graduation, even though there is no military obligation on your part while in college—no drills, no uniforms, no special classes.

After graduation you spend four months in Navy Officer Candidate School. Following receipt of your commission you are obligated to spend five years on active duty with the Navy. This program will contribute over $30,000 toward your education if you sign up at the beginning of your sophomore year.

For additional information on these programs visit your local Navy recruiting office.

The Air Force Reserve Officers Training Corps. High school seniors interested in becoming Air Force officers should seek an AFROTC scholarship. These scholarships are awarded on a competitive basis to high school seniors or graduates who want to major in selected technical and scientific areas. These include engineering, mathematics, meteorology, and computer science. As you can see, this program is primarily for science and engineering majors. Few scholarships are ever available in other areas.

General Eligibility Requirements

1. You must be a citizen of the United States.
2. You must graduate from high school or hold an equivalent certificate.
3. You must be at least 17 years old when you enter the program, and less than 25 when you complete it.
4. You must not be (or have been) enrolled as a full-time student in a junior college or university except for joint high school college programs.
5. You must meet the Air Force's physical standards.
6. You must be accepted not only by a college or university that is affiliated with AFROTC, but by the department in that school offering the academic major for which the scholarship has been awarded. In other words, if your scholarship has been awarded to you as an engineering major, you must be accepted into the college's engineering department to use the scholarship.
7. You must have a high school grade-point average of at least 2.5 and have been in the top 25 percent of your class. These can be waived if you are enrolled in an honors or advanced program.
8. You must have minimum SAT scores of 500 math and 450 verbal or ACT minimums of 20 in math and 19 in English.

Academic Requirements

1. You must complete all requirements for a bachelor's degree in the major for which the scholarship was awarded, in accordance with the college or university's rules.

2. You must successfully complete one year of college instruction in a major Indo-European or Asian language.
3. Regardless of your academic major you are required to take part in your ROTC unit's drills and successfully complete the following courses, for which you will receive credit. The amount of credit depends on the policies of the college.

> The Air Force Today
> The Development of Airpower
> Air Force Leadership and Management
> National Security Forces in Contemporary American Society

In addition all cadets must attend the Leadership Laboratory, which involves the cadet in the planning and operation of the ROTC unit.
4. You must successfully complete one four-week summer training session.

If you are selected as a finalist in the competition, you will be required to complete an application that includes your high school transcript, teacher recommendations, and a report on your extracurricular activities. You will then be interviewed by a panel of Air Force officers and take a medical examination.

Military Service Requirements. After graduation as an AFROTC cadet you will be expected to:

1. Accept a commission in the Air Force, if offered.
2. Serve at least four years active duty with the Air Force.

For additional information and scholarship applications, a list of colleges affiliated with the Air Force ROTC, as well as a schedule of closing dates for the coming year, either visit the AFROTC unit on a campus near you or write:

> Public Affairs Office
> Air Force ROTC
> Maxwell AFB, AL 36112-6663

Other Air Force Programs

Two-Year Scholarships. The Air Force also has a two-year scholarship program with many of the same benefits as the four-year program outlined above. It is open to college students completing their sophomore year at a four-year college or to those transferring from a two-year college. As with the four-year scholarships, these are generally awarded to students majoring in science or engineering. Students accepted are required to attend a summer training session of six weeks' duration before starting their junior year. This time is spent to bring them up to date with the training they missed the first two years. This requirement is waived for students who have already been nonscholarship ROTC cadets.

Nonscholarship AFROTC. The Air Force offers both four- and two-year nonscholarship ROTC programs that are similar to the scholarship programs, except they don't pay for your tuition or for books other than those used for ROTC classes. In addition, the $100 monthly tax-free allowance is only available during the student's junior and senior years. The active duty requirement for nonscholarship cadets is three years.

Premed/Medical Nursing Program. Premed and nursing students can compete for either two- or four-year scholarships with the same benefits already outlined. Nursing graduates are commissioned as second lieutenants in the Air Force Nurse Corps. The same benefits are guaranteed through medical school, except for a higher monthly allowance, on acceptance at an accredited school of medicine.

College Senior Engineering Program. Limited to engineering majors in their junior or senior year at college this program generally selects fewer than 100 of several thousand applicants each year. Those selected are enlisted as Airman First Class and earn commensurate pay until they receive their bachelor's degree. The current salary is approximately $750 per month. There is no obligation while you are attending college, but after graduation you will be assigned to Officer Training School for about three months. Successful completion leads to a commission as a second lieutenant. You then begin your four-year active duty obligation. Your assignment will be in the engineering field in which you majored.

For additional information on these programs visit your local Air Force recruiting office.

Army Reserve Officers Training Corps. High school seniors interested in becoming Army officers should seek an AROTC scholarship. These scholarships are awarded on a competitive basis to high school seniors or graduates. More than 60 percent of the awards are reserved for students majoring in engineering, the physical sciences, nursing, and other technical fields.

General Eligibility Requirements

1. You must be a citizen when the award is accepted.
2. You must be at least 17 years old by October 1 of the year the scholarship becomes effective.
3. You must graduate from high school, but not yet be enrolled in college.
4. You must be accepted by a college or university that hosts an AROTC unit. At present, students attending cross-enrollment colleges are not eligible for four-year scholarships, but this policy is under review and may change soon.
5. Your combined minimum SAT scores (math and verbal) must be 850, or you must have a minimum ACT score (math and English) of 17.
6. You must have good high school grades and have participated in leadership, extracurricular, and athletic activities. (Those students who hold part-time jobs and do not have enough time to participate in these activities will be awarded credit in these areas based on the number of hours worked each week.)
7. You must agree to accept a commission as an officer in either the Regular Army, Army National Guard, or Army Reserve, whichever is offered.

Academic Requirements

1. You must complete all requirements for a bachelor's degree in the major for which the scholarship was awarded, in accordance with the rules of the college or university.
2. You must successfully complete at least one quarter or semester of college instruction in a major Indo-European or Asian language.
3. You must maintain acceptable academic standards and place in the top half of your ROTC class, which will also contain nonscholarship students.
4. You must successfully complete one six-week summer training session.
5. Regardless of your academic major, you are required to take part in your ROTC unit's drills and successfully complete the mandatory military-science courses.

If you are selected as a finalist in the competition, you will be required to complete an application that includes your high school transcript, teacher recommendations, and a report on your extracurricular activities. You will then be interviewed by a panel of Army officers and take a medical examination.

Military Service Requirements. After graduation as an Army ROTC cadet you will be expected to:

1. Accept a commission in either the Regular Army, Army National Guard, or Army Reserve, whichever is offered.
2. Your active duty obligation will vary depending on your commission. You can serve two to four years on active duty as an officer in the Regular Army, followed by service in the Army National Guard, or three to six months active duty and eight years in the Reserves. Your commission will depend on the Army's needs at the time.

For additional information and scholarship applications, a list of Army ROTC "host" colleges, as well as closing dates for the coming year, either visit the Army ROTC unit on a campus near you, or write:

Army ROTC
Post Office Box 9000
Clifton, NJ 07015-9974

Other Army Programs

Two- and Three-Year Scholarships. The Army also has a two- and three-year scholarship program with many of the same benefits as the four-year program outlined above. It is open to college students completing their freshman or sophomore year at a four-year college or to those transferring from a two-year college. Students accepted are required to attend a special six-week basic training camp during the summer. This time is spent to bring them up to date with the training they missed. This requirement is waived for students who have already been nonscholarship ROTC cadets.

Nonscholarship AROTC. The Army offers both two- and four-year nonscholarship ROTC programs that are similar to the scholarship programs, except the Army pays only for tuition and books related to your ROTC classes. Nonscholarship cadets have the opportunity to be awarded a scholarship during their participation in the basic camp summer training. The active military obligation for nonscholarship participants in Army ROTC is three years.

To learn which colleges and universities participate in Army, Navy, or Air Force ROTC programs see the Appendix, *College Profiles for Cost Cutters.*

of the traditional colleges and universities included in the Appendix, *College Profiles for Cost Cutters.*

Each institution offering external degree programs has its own policy concerning how credits may be earned and how much time must actually be spent on the campus. Readers who want more detailed information about external degree programs from specific colleges and universities can write the institutions directly. The information is also available in my previous book, *How to Earn a College Degree Without Going to College.*

How Much Time on Campus? Since the Regents and Edison external degree programs have no campuses, students enrolled in either don't have to spend time on campus. Among other traditional colleges and universities there are three approaches to this question. At some colleges the student isn't required to spend any time at the institution, except possibly for attending graduation. Others require their external degree program students to visit the college for a limited time, perhaps one day spent meeting a faculty advisor or attending a seminar explaining how the program works and introducing the external degree program staff to the students.

Still others require students to attend traditional classes for a specific amount of time, generally enough to earn 25 percent of the credits required for the student's degree. This last policy means an external degree student can earn the equivalent of three years' worth of credits but must spend the final year on campus attending classes.

How Credits Are Earned. Excluding credits that might have to be earned through traditional classes, external degree students are generally able to earn their credits from any source that is recognized or accredited by a regional accrediting agency.

Most external degree programs permit their students to apply credits toward a degree from the following sources:

- Courses taken for credit at regionally accredited colleges and universities. Noncredit courses cannot be used. A transcript must be sent from the college at which the courses were taken to your external degree program college.
- Correspondence courses offered for college credit by a regionally accredited college or university. Chapter 5 describes how correspondence courses work. It also contains a list of colleges and

universities that offer correspondence courses for credit and the subjects available through correspondence.

- Credits earned through proficiency examinations. Chapter 7 contains complete information on two national proficiency examination programs: CLEP and PEP. In addition, some programs offer their own examinations, such as the Thomas Edison College Examination Program, the Regents College Examinations, the Ohio University Examination Program, and the University of North Carolina Examination Program. Some of these examinations are recognized for credit by external degree programs from other institutions.

  Many external degree programs will also award credits for passing Advanced Placement Examinations, Graduate Record Examinations, and tests administered by the Defense Activity for Non-Traditional Education Support (DANTES). You must review which examinations are eligible for credit from the external degree program in which you are interested in enrolling.

- Noncollege courses offered by businesses, government agencies, associations, unions, and other groups, provided the courses have been evaluated and recommended for credit by the Program on Non-collegiate Sponsored Instruction (PONSI) of the American Council on Education.
- Military courses and programs that have been evaluated and recommended for credit by PONSI.
- Selected professional licenses and certificates that are issued by public agencies, such as Federal Aviation Administration licenses.
- Special assessments of the knowledge you've gained through your life experience. There are several forms this type of assessment of your knowledge may take. For detailed information see Chapter 6, *Earning Credit for What You Already Know.*

Not every external degree program will award credit for every method mentioned here. If there are certain methods you want to use, be sure they are acceptable to the program you're interested in before you enroll.

The Value of Your External Degree. The diploma awarded by an external degree program looks exactly like any other degree conferred by that institution. Many people for whom an external degree program might be the answer to reaching their educational goals fear the degree they will work so hard to earn will not be as good as one earned through traditional methods. This isn't the case. The diploma itself doesn't refer to the methods you used to earn credits. In those instances where you must submit a transcript that might reveal your use of alternative education, such as applying to a graduate school, it usually has no effect on your acceptance.

What It Costs. The cost of earning your college degree through an external degree program varies depending on the methods used to earn credit. If you prefer to attend traditional college classes to earn most of your credits, the cost will be higher than if you choose proficiency examinations. It is possible in some cases to earn your degree for less than $1,000.

Selecting the Right Program. To find the external degree program that best meets your needs and goals, and fits your lifestyle, contact colleges and universities offering external degree programs. Read through the literature they send you. If you already have credit from previous college courses, be sure the programs that interest you will accept the transfer of those credits. This is especially important if the credits were earned over five years ago.

Next decide what alternative education methods you would use to earn additional credits. When you've made your decision, be sure the programs that interest you will accept credits earned by those methods.

A major factor to keep in mind is whether or not you have to spend time on campus. If for whatever reason you won't be able to attend traditional classes, no matter how flexible the schedule, then you are wise to consider only those programs that are truly external and don't require your attendance at classes or seminars.

Colleges Without Campuses. The Appendix, *College Profiles for Cost Cutters,* will show you which traditional colleges and universities offer external degree programs. The two institutions that have no campuses or classes are listed below. If you are considering earning your college degree through an external degree program, you should include both of these institutions in your decision-making process.

Regents College Degrees
The University of the State of New York
Cultural Education Center
Albany, NY 12230
(518) 474-3703

Thomas A. Edison State College
101 West State Street
Trenton, NJ 08625
(609) 984-1150

APPENDIX

COLLEGE PROFILES FOR COST CUTTERS

Throughout this book we discussed ways in which you can reduce the cost of a college education. The following unique directory of American colleges and universities shows you where you can use as many of these cost-cutting methods as possible. The directory includes the names and locations of over 1,500 colleges and universities, and shows you which cost-cutting methods are available at each institution.

How to Use the College Profiles. If you have already prepared a list of colleges from which you plan to make your final selection, check to see how many are included in the list given here. Each college and university is arranged alphabetically by state.

When you find a college from your list in the profiles, place a ruler under that college's entry and read across the columns to the right. Each column has a heading identifying a single cost-cutting method. A dot in a particular column means the college you are checking offers that method. Highlight those colleges on your list offering the cost-cutting methods you want to use to reduce your college costs.

Other factors aside, if you are serious about cutting your college costs, those colleges and universities offering you the opportunity to save money should be given priority. Contact each college directly and ask for specific information about policies relating to the cost-cutting methods you want to use.

The following are descriptions of the headings for the columns in the profiles.

External Degrees. External degree programs permit students to attain a college degree primarily by alternative means of earning credits. Most external degree programs require no time spent on campus, although a small number of colleges do require external degree candidates to attend a seminar or meeting on campus before conferring a degree. Information on external degree programs can be found in Chapter 11.

Work-Study. This is a government-sponsored program that provides part-time jobs for college students to help them pay for their education. The amount of money you can earn is limited, and participation in the program requires proof of financial need. Work-study income is usually included as part of a student's financial aid package. See Chapter 9 for additional details.

Correspondence Courses. Some colleges and universities now award full credit for successful completion of correspondence courses. These require no classroom attendance and can be taken by students living thousands of miles from the college's campus. They can also be taken for credit by those attending the college as resident students. Often a student can reduce the amount of time required to earn a bachelor's degree by one full year through correspondence courses. For complete information see Chapter 5.

Life Experience. Students can be awarded credit by demonstrating the college-level knowledge they've acquired through their own life experiences. This knowledge can be based on almost any type of experience, including work, hobbies, reading, and noncredit courses. See Chapter 6 for more details.

Proficiency Exams. These examinations test a student's knowledge in selected subjects that correspond to college courses. Those receiving a passing grade can be awarded credit without taking the course. Many colleges permit a student to save a year or more in school by using these examinations. Detailed information on proficiency examinations for credit can be found in Chapter 7.

Co-op Programs. Co-operative education programs permit a student to combine study with work in the same field in which the student is majoring. Some colleges offer co-op programs through certain departments only, so you should contact those colleges you're interested in to find out if the co-op program is offered for your major. Chapter 9 provides additional details on co-op programs.

Federal Co-op. These co-operative education programs are conducted with most agencies of the federal government. Many can lead to job offers for those interested in working for the government. See Chapter 9 for more information.

Guaranteed Tuition. An approach to paying for college that is receiving increased attention and participation, guaranteed tuition programs generally set a student's tuition for the four years of college at the student's entry year tuition rate. This saves the student the tuition increases that can be expected each of the following years. Some of these programs also include other costs, such as board and fees. See Chapter 3 for more details on these programs.

Accelerated Degrees. To help highly qualified students reduce the time it takes to earn a degree by as much as one year, some colleges will permit them to accelerate their learning through increased classes during each semester or by attending classes during the summer months. Chapter 3 provides additional details.

Advanced Placement. High school students can save up to one year of college by attending special courses preparing them for a series of tests known as the Advanced Placement Program. Those successfully passing the tests receive college credit instead of having to attend the corresponding freshman class. The colleges and universities with a dot in this column have reported that they will award credit to incoming students with acceptable grades in Advanced Placement examinations. Chapter 8 has additional details.

ROTC. Scholarships provided through ROTC programs of the Army, Navy, and Air Force can drastically reduce the cost of earning a college degree. While some colleges have ROTC units on campus, others have agreements to permit their students to join an ROTC unit at a nearby campus of another institution. An A in this column means the institution participates in the Army ROTC. An N means participation in the Navy ROTC which includes Marine officer candidates. Participation in the Air Force ROTC is indicated by AF. For more information on all ROTC programs, see Chapter 10.

	External Degrees	Work-Study	Correspondence Courses	Life Experience	Proficiency Exams	Co-op Programs	Federal Co-op	Guaranteed Tuition	Accelerated Degrees	Advanced Placement	ROTC
ALABAMA											
Alabama A&M University Normal	•				•	•	•		•	•	A
Alabama State University Montgomery	•				•	•	•		•		AF
Athens State College Athens			•	•	•	•	•				
Auburn University Auburn	•	•			•	•			•	•	A N AF
Auburn University/Montgomery	•				•	•	•		•		AF
Birmingham–Southern College Birmingham	•		•	•	•				•	•	AF
Faulkner University Montgomery					•	•					
Huntingdon College Montgomery	•		•	•	•	•				•	AF
Jacksonville State University				•	•	•	•		•	•	A
Judson College Marion	•				•	•			•	•	
Livingston University Livingston	•		•	•	•				•	•	
Miles College Birmingham					•		•				AF
Mobile College Mobile	•				•				•	•	
Oakwood College Huntsville	•		•	•	•	•	•		•	•	
Samford University Birmingham	•				•	•			•	•	AF
Southeastern Bible College Birmingham					•						
Spring Hill College Mobile	•				•				•	•	
Stillman College Tuscaloosa	•				•	•	•		•	•	
Talladega College Talladega	•				•	•	•		•		
Troy State University Troy	•		•		•	•			•	•	AF
Troy State University/Dothan	•				•				•		

	External Degrees	Work-Study	Correspondence Courses	Life Experience	Proficiency Exams	Co-op Programs	Federal Co-op	Guaranteed Tuition	Accelerated Degrees	Advanced Placement	ROTC
Troy State University/Montgomery		•			•				•		AF
Tuskegee University Tuskegee		•	•	•	•	•	•			•	A AF
University of Alabama Tuscaloosa	•		•	•	•	•	•		•	•	A AF
University of Alabama/Birmingham		•		•	•	•	•		•	•	A AF
University of Alabama/Huntsville		•			•	•			•		
University of Montevallo					•	•			•	•	AF
University of North Alabama Florence		•			•	•				•	A
University of South Alabama Mobile		•			•	•	•		•	•	A AF
ALASKA											
Alaska Pacific University Anchorage	•	•		•	•	•			•	•	
Sheldon Jackson College Sitka		•		•	•	•					
University of Alaska/Anchorage		•			•		•			•	
University of Alaska/Fairbanks			•		•		•			•	A
University of Alaska/Juneau		•			•	•				•	
ARIZONA											
Arizona State University Tempe		•	•	•	•	•	•		•	•	A AF
Devry Institute of Technology Phoenix						•			•		AF
Embry-Riddle Aeronautical University Prescott		•		•	•	•			•	•	AF
Grand Canyon College Phoenix		•			•				•	•	AF
Northern Arizona University Flagstaff		•		•	•	•	•		•	•	A AF
Prescott College Prescott	•			•	•	•			•		

	External Degrees	Work-Study	Correspondence Courses	Life Experience	Proficiency Exams	Co-op Programs	Federal Co-op	Guaranteed Tuition	Accelerated Degrees	Advanced Placement	ROTC
Southwestern Baptist Bible College Phoenix					•					•	
University of Arizona Tucson	•	•			•	•	•			•	A N AF
University of Phoenix				•	•		•		•		
Western International University Phoenix	•					•		•	•		
ARKANSAS											
Arkansas Baptist College Little Rock	•										
Arkansas College Batesville	•				•	•				•	
Arkansas State University State University	•	•	•	•	•				•	•	A
Arkansas State University/Beebe					•				•	•	
Arkansas Tech University Russellville	•				•		•			•	A
Central Baptist College Conway	•							•			
College of the Ozarks Clarksville	•				•	•					
Harding University Searcy					•	•			•	•	
Henderson State University Arkadelphia	•				•	•			•	•	A AF
Hendrix College Conway	•				•				•	•	
John Brown University Siloam Springs	•			•	•					•	
Ouachita Baptist University Arkadelphia	•				•	•				•	A
Southern Arkansas University Magnolia	•				•				•	•	A AF
University of Arkansas Fayetteville	•	•			•	•			•	•	A AF
University of Arkansas/Little Rock	•		•	•			•		•	•	A AF

	External Degrees	Work-Study	Correspondence Courses	Life Experience	Proficiency Exams	Co-op Programs	Federal Co-op	Guaranteed Tuition	Accelerated Degrees	Advanced Placement	ROTC
University of Arkansas/Monticello		•		•	•		•		•	•	A AF
University of Arkansas/Pine Bluff		•			•	•	•		•	•	A AF
University of Central Arkansas Conway		•			•	•			•	•	A AF
CALIFORNIA											
Ambassador College Pasadena					•				•		
Armstrong University Berkeley	•	•		•	•				•	•	
Art Center College of Design Pasadena					•						
Azusa Pacific College Azusa		•			•	•			•	•	
Biola University La Mirada		•			•				•	•	N AF
Brooks Institute Santa Barbara		•			•				•	•	
California Baptist College Riverside		•		•	•				•	•	
California College of Arts & Crafts Oakland		•		•	•	•			•	•	
California Institute of Technology Pasadena		•							•		N AF
California Institute of the Arts Valencia		•			•				•	•	
California Lutheran University Thousand Oaks		•			•	•			•	•	AF
California Maritime Academy Vallejo		•			•				•	•	N
California Polytech State Univ. San Luis Obispo		•			•	•	•			•	A AF
California State College Bakersfield	•	•		•	•	•	•		•	•	
California State Polytech Univ. Pomona		•			•	•	•		•	•	A N AF
California State Univ./Chico	•	•		•	•	•	•		•	•	

	External Degrees	Work-Study	Correspondence Courses	Life Experience	Proficiency Exams	Co-op Programs	Federal Co-op	Guaranteed Tuition	Accelerated Degrees	Advanced Placement	ROTC
California State Univ./Dominguez Hills Carson	•	•		•	•	•			•	•	AF
California State Univ./Fresno		•		•	•	•			•	•	A AF
California State Univ./Fullerton		•		•	•	•			•	•	A N AF
California State Univ./Hayward	•	•		•	•	•			•	•	N AF
California State Univ./Long Beach	•	•		•	•	•				•	A N AF
California State Univ./Los Angeles		•		•	•	•			•	•	N AF
California State Univ./Northridge		•		•	•	•			•	•	N AF
California State Univ./Sacramento		•	•	•	•	•				•	N AF
California State Univ./San Bernardino		•		•	•	•				•	A AF
California State Univ./Stanislaus Turlock	•	•		•	•				•	•	
Chapman College Orange		•		•	•				•	•	AF
Christ College/Irvine				•	•						
Christian Heritage College El Cajon				•					•		
Claremont McKenna College Claremont		•							•	•	A AF
Cogswell College San Francisco		•	•	•	•				•	•	
College of Notre Dame Belmont		•		•	•				•	•	
Dominican College of San Rafael San Rafael		•	•	•	•				•		
Fresno Pacific College Fresno		•		•					•		
Golden Gate University San Francisco		•		•	•	•			•	•	
Harvey Mudd College Claremont		•							•	•	N AF

	External Degrees	Work-Study	Correspondence Courses	Life Experience	Proficiency Exams	Co-op Programs	Federal Co-op	Guaranteed Tuition	Accelerated Degrees	Advanced Placement	ROTC
Holy Names College Oakland		•			•					•	AF
Humboldt State University Arcata		•	•		•	•			•	•	
Humphreys College Stockton					•					•	
Loma Linda University		•			•					•	
Loyola Marymount University Los Angeles		•			•					•	N AF
Menlo College Menlo Park						•			•	•	
Master's College Newhall					•					•	
Mills College Oakland		•			•		•		•	•	AF
Monterey Institute of International Studies Monterey					•	•				•	
Mount St. Mary's College Los Angeles		•		•	•					•	
National University San Diego		•		•	•		•			•	AF
New College of California San Francisco		•		•	•	•			•	•	
Northrop University Inglewood		•				•	•		•	•	N AF
Occidental College Los Angeles		•							•	•	N AF
Otis Art Institute Los Angeles		•			•					•	
Pacific Christian College Fullerton	•	•		•	•				•	•	
Pacific Union College Angwin		•			•				•	•	
Patten College Oakland		•			•					•	
Pepperdine University Malibu	•	•			•				•	•	AF
Pitzer College Claremont		•								•	
Point Loma College San Diego		•			•				•	•	N AF

	External Degrees	Work-Study	Correspondence Courses	Life Experience	Proficiency Exams	Co-op Programs	Federal Co-op	Guaranteed Tuition	Accelerated Degrees	Advanced Placement	ROTC
Pomona College Claremont										•	AF
Saint Mary's College of California Moraga	•			•	•			•		•	AF
San Diego State University	•	•			•	•	•			•	A N AF
San Francisco Art Institute		•			•				•	•	
San Francisco Conservatory of Music		•			•				•	•	
San Francisco State University	•	•		•	•	•			•	•	N
San Jose Bible College		•		•	•				•		
San Jose State University	•	•			•	•	•		•	•	A N AF
Santa Clara University		•				•		•		•	A N AF
Scripps College Claremont		•			•					•	
Simpson College San Francisco		•			•				•	•	
Sonoma State University Rohnert Park		•		•	•		•			•	AF
Southern California College Costa Mesa		•			•				•	•	
Stanford University Stanford		•					•		•	•	N
United States International Univ. San Diego		•			•				•	•	
University of California/Berkeley		•	•			•	•		•	•	A N AF
University of California/Davis		•				•	•		•	•	A N AF
University of California/Irvine	•	•					•		•	•	N AF
University of California/Los Angeles	•	•				•	•			•	A N AF
University of California/Riverside		•				•	•		•	•	AF
University of California/San Diego La Jolla	•	•				•	•		•	•	AF

	External Degrees	Work-Study	Correspondence Courses	Life Experience	Proficiency Exams	Co-op Programs	Federal Co-op	Guaranteed Tuition	Accelerated Degrees	Advanced Placement	ROTC
University of California/Santa Barbara		•			•		•		•	•	A AF
University of California/Santa Cruz	•	•				•	•		•		
University of Judaism Los Angeles		•			•				•	•	
University of La Verne	•	•	•	•	•	•			•	•	AF
University of Redlands	•	•	•	•					•	•	AF
University of San Diego		•								•	N AF
University of San Francisco	•	•		•	•	•			•	•	A N
University of Southern California Los Angeles		•		•	•	•	•	•	•	•	A N AF
University of the Pacific Stockton	•	•		•	•	•			•	•	A N
West Coast Christian College Fresno		•		•	•					•	AF
West Coast University Los Angeles					•				•	•	
Westmont College Santa Barbara		•			•	•			•	•	AF
Whittier College Whittier		•			•				•	•	AF
Woodbury University Los Angeles		•			•				•	•	
World College West San Rafael		•				•					
COLORADO											
Adams State College Alamosa		•	•		•		•		•	•	
Colorado College Colorado Springs		•							•		
Colorado School of Mines Golden		•			•	•	•		•	•	A
Colorado State University Fort Collins		•	•	•	•	•	•			•	A AF
Colorado Technical College Colorado Springs	•	•		•	•				•	•	
Fort Lewis College Durango		•		•	•	•	•		•	•	

	External Degrees	Work-Study	Correspondence Courses	Life Experience	Proficiency Exams	Co-op Programs	Federal Co-op	Guaranteed Tuition	Accelerated Degrees	Advanced Placement	ROTC
Loretto Heights College Denver	•	•		•	•	•			•	•	
Mesa College Grand Junction		•		•	•	•					A
Metropolitan State College Denver		•		•	•	•	•		•	•	A AF
Regis College Denver		•		•	•	•			•	•	AF
Rockmont College Denver				•	•		•		•		
University of Colorado/Boulder Boulder		•	•	•	•	•			•	•	A N AF
University of Colorado/Colorado Springs		•		•	•				•	•	A
University of Colorado/Denver		•		•	•	•			•	•	AF
University of Denver		•		•	•				•	•	
University of Northern Colorado Greeley	•	•	•	•	•	•			•	•	AF
University of Southern Colorado Pueblo		•	•	•	•	•	•		•	•	A
Western State College of Colorado Gunnison		•			•				•	•	
CONNECTICUT											
Albertus Magnus College New Haven		•		•	•					•	
Central Connecticut State University New Britain		•				•	•				AF
Connecticut College New London		•						•	•	•	
Eastern Connecticut State University Willimantic		•		•	•				•	•	AF
Fairfield University Fairfield		•		•	•					•	
Post College Waterbury		•		•	•				•	•	

	External Degrees	Work-Study	Correspondence Courses	Life Experience	Proficiency Exams	Co-op Programs	Federal Co-op	Guaranteed Tuition	Accelerated Degrees	Advanced Placement	ROTC
Quinnipiac College Hamden	•	•		•	•				•	•	
Sacred Heart University Bridgeport		•	•	•	•				•	•	
Saint Alphonsus College Suffield				•	•					•	
Saint Joseph College West Hartford		•		•	•			•	•	•	AF
Southern Connecticut State University New Haven		•		•	•				•	•	AF
Trinity College Hartford	•	•							•	•	AF
University of Bridgeport		•	•	•	•	•	•		•	•	A
University of Connecticut Storrs	•	•		•	•	•			•	•	A AF
University of Hartford West Hartford		•	•	•	•	•	•			•	AF
University of New Haven West Haven		•		•	•	•			•	•	
Wesleyan University Middletown		•			•				•	•	AF
Western Connecticut State University Danbury		•	•	•	•				•	•	AF
Yale University New Haven		•					•	•	•	•	AF
DELAWARE											
Delaware State College Dover		•	•	•		•				•	AF
Goldey Beacom College Wilmington		•		•	•				•	•	
University of Delaware Newark		•		•	•				•	•	A AF
Wesley College Dover		•		•	•				•	•	
Widener University Wilmington		•		•	•				•		
Wilmington College New Castle		•	•	•	•				•	•	AF

	External Degrees	Work-Study	Correspondence Courses	Life Experience	Proficiency Exams	Co-op Programs	Federal Co-op	Guaranteed Tuition	Accelerated Degrees	Advanced Placement	ROTC
DISTRICT OF COLUMBIA											
American University Washington	•	•		•	•	•	•			•	N AF
Beacon College Washington	•			•	•	•				•	
Benjamin Franklin University Washington					•				•	•	
Catholic University of America Washington		•		•	•	•			•	•	N AF
Gallaudet College Washington		•		•	•	•			•	•	
George Washington University Washington		•		•	•	•		•	•	•	N AF
Georgetown University Washington		•		•	•					•	A N AF
Howard University Washington	•	•	•	•	•	•	•		•	•	A N AF
Mount Vernon College Washington		•		•	•				•	•	
Southeastern University Washington		•		•	•				•		
Strayer College Washington		•		•	•				•	•	
Trinity College Washington		•		•	•				•	•	AF
University of the District of Columbia Washington		•		•	•	•				•	N AF
FLORIDA											
Baptist Bible Institute Graceville				•					•		
Barry University Miami Shores		•		•	•				•	•	AF
Bethune-Cookman College Daytona Beach		•		•	•	•			•	•	AF
College of Boca Raton				•	•				•	•	
Eckerd College St. Petersburg	•	•		•	•	•			•	•	
Edward Waters College Jacksonville					•	•					

	External Degrees	Work-Study	Correspondence Courses	Life Experience	Proficiency Exams	Co-op Programs	Federal Co-op	Guaranteed Tuition	Accelerated Degrees	Advanced Placement	ROTC
Embry-Riddle Aeronautical University Daytona Beach	•	•		•	•	•	•		•	•	A AF
Flagler College St. Augustine		•		•	•					•	
Florida A&M University Tallahassee		•		•	•	•			•	•	A N AF
Florida Atlantic University Boca Raton		•		•	•	•			•	•	AF
Florida Institute of Technology Melbourne		•				•	•		•	•	A
Florida International University Miami	•	•		•	•	•			•	•	AF
Florida Memorial College Miami				•	•	•					AF
Florida Southern College Lakeland		•			•					•	A AF
Florida State University Tallahassee		•		•	•	•			•	•	A N AF
Fort Lauderdale College Ft. Lauderdale		•		•	•				•		
Jacksonville University				•				•	•	•	N
Jones College/Jacksonville		•		•					•		
Miami Christian College Miami		•		•					•	•	
Nova University Ft. Lauderdale	•	•	•	•	•				•	•	
Orlando College Orlando		•		•	•				•	•	A AF
Palm Beach Atlantic College West Palm Beach		•		•					•		
Ringling School of Art Sarasota		•		•					•		
Rollins College Winter Park		•		•					•	•	
St. John Vianney College Seminary Miami				•						•	
Saint Leo College Saint Leo	•	•		•					•	•	A AF
St. Thomas University Miami	•	•		•	•	•				•	

	External Degrees	Work-Study	Correspondence Courses	Life Experience	Proficiency Exams	Co-op Programs	Federal Co-op	Guaranteed Tuition	Accelerated Degrees	Advanced Placement	ROTC
Southeastern College of the Assemblies of God Lakeland		•		•	•				•	•	
Stetson University Deland		•			•	•			•	•	A
Tampa College					•				•		
University of Central Florida Orlando		•			•	•	•		•	•	A AF
University of Florida Gainesville		•	•		•	•	•		•	•	A N AF
University of Miami Coral Gables		•		•	•	•	•	•	•	•	A AF
University of North Florida Jacksonville		•			•	•	•			•	A N
University of South Florida St. Petersburg				•	•					•	A
University of South Florida Tampa	•	•		•	•	•	•		•	•	A AF
University of South Florida Sarasota		•							•		
University of Tampa		•		•	•					•	A AF
University of West Florida Pensacola		•			•	•	•		•	•	
Warner Southern College Lake Wales		•			•				•	•	
Webber College Babson Park		•		•	•				•		
GEORGIA											
Agnes Scott College Decatur		•							•	•	N AF
Albany State College Albany		•			•	•	•			•	A
Armstrong State College Savannah			•	•	•	•	•		•	•	A N
Atlanta Christian College East Point		•		•							
Atlanta College of Art		•								•	
Augusta State College Augusta		•			•	•	•		•	•	A

	External Degrees	Work-Study	Correspondence Courses	Life Experience	Proficiency Exams	Co-op Programs	Federal Co-op	Guaranteed Tuition	Accelerated Degrees	Advanced Placement	ROTC
Berry College Mount Berry		•			•	•	•		•	•	A
Brenau College Gainesville		•	•	•		•			•	•	
Clark College Atlanta		•			•	•			•		N AF
Columbus College Columbus		•			•	•			•	•	A
Covenant College Lookout Mountain	•	•		•					•	•	
Devry Institute of Technology Atlanta		•					•		•		
Emory University Atlanta		•							•	•	
Fort Valley State College Fort Valley		•			•	•	•			•	A
Georgia College Milledgeville		•	•	•	•	•	•		•	•	
Georgia Institute of Technology Atlanta		•				•	•		•	•	A N AF
Georgia Southern College Statesboro		•	•	•	•	•				•	A
Georgia Southwestern College Americus		•		•	•	•			•	•	A
Georgia State University Atlanta		•	•	•	•	•	•		•	•	A N AF
Kennesaw College Marietta		•			•	•			•	•	N
LaGrange College LaGrange		•		•					•		
Mercer University Macon		•		•					•	•	A
Mercer University in Atlanta		•	•	•			•		•	•	
Morehouse College Atlanta		•				•	•				N AF
Morris Brown College Atlanta		•			•	•	•		•	•	N AF
North Georgia College Dahlonega		•	•	•						•	A
Oglethorpe University Atlanta		•			•	•		•	•	•	N

	External Degrees	Work-Study	Correspondence Courses	Life Experience	Proficiency Exams	Co-op Programs	Federal Co-op	Guaranteed Tuition	Accelerated Degrees	Advanced Placement	ROTC
Paine College Augusta		•		•	•	•	•		•	•	
Piedmont College Demorest		•			•				•	•	
Savannah College of Art & Design Savannah		•			•				•		
Savannah State College Savannah		•			•	•	•		•		N
Shorter College Rome		•			•				•	•	
Southern Technical Institute Marietta		•			•	•			•	•	N AF
Spelman College Atlanta		•			•	•			•	•	N AF
Tift College Forsyth		•			•	•			•	•	
Toccoa Falls College Toccoa Falls		•			•				•	•	
University of Georgia Athens		•	•		•	•	•		•	•	A AF
Valdosta State College Valdosta		•			•	•	•		•	•	AF
Wesleyan College Macon		•		•	•			•	•	•	
West Georgia College Carrollton	•	•			•	•	•		•	•	
HAWAII											
Brigham Young University–Hawaii Laie, Oahu				•	•	•			•	•	AF
Chaminade University of Honolulu		•		•	•	•	•		•	•	AF
Hawaii Loa College Kaneohe		•			•				•	•	AF
Hawaii Pacific College Honolulu		•			•	•			•	•	AF
University of Hawaii at Hilo		•			•	•	•		•	•	
University of Hawaii at Manoa Honolulu		•			•	•	•		•	•	A AF

	External Degrees	Work-Study	Correspondence Courses	Life Experience	Proficiency Exams	Co-op Programs	Federal Co-op	Guaranteed Tuition	Accelerated Degrees	Advanced Placement	ROTC
IDAHO											
Boise State University Boise		•	•		•		•			•	A
College of Idaho Caldwell		•			•			•		•	
Idaho State University Pocatello		•	•		•		•			•	A
Lewis-Clark State College Lewiston		•	•	•	•	•	•		•	•	
Northwest Nazarene College Nampa		•			•				•	•	
University of Idaho Moscow		•	•	•	•	•	•		•	•	A N AF
ILLINOIS											
American Conservatory of Music Chicago		•			•				•	•	
Augustana College Rock Island		•					•		•	•	
Aurora University Aurora		•		•	•					•	
Barat College Lake Forest		•		•	•				•	•	
Blackburn College Carlinville		•			•	•			•	•	
Bradley University Peoria		•			•	•	•		•	•	A
Chicago State University	•	•		•	•	•	•		•	•	A AF
College of St. Francis Joliet	•	•		•	•	•			•	•	
Columbia College Chicago		•		•	•	•			•	•	
Concordia College River Forest		•			•		•		•	•	
Delourdes College Des Plaines					•						
DePaul University Chicago	•	•		•	•		•		•	•	
Devry Institute of Technology Chicago		•				•			•		

	External Degrees	Work-Study	Correspondence Courses	Life Experience	Proficiency Exams	Co-op Programs	Federal Co-op	Guaranteed Tuition	Accelerated Degrees	Advanced Placement	ROTC
Eastern Illinois University Charleston	•	•		•	•	•	•			•	A
Elmhurst College Elmhurst		•		•	•	•			•	•	N AF
Eureka College Eureka		•		•	•	•	•		•	•	
Greenville College Greenville		•			•				•		
Illinois Benedictine College Lisle		•		•	•	•					
Illinois College Jacksonville		•			•				•	•	
Illinois Institute of Technology Chicago		•				•	•		•	•	N AF
Illinois State University Normal		•		•	•	•	•		•	•	A
Illinois Wesleyan University Bloomington		•			•				•	•	
Judson College Elgin		•		•	•				•	•	
Kendall College Evanston		•			•					•	
Knox College Galesburg		•			•				•	•	A
Lake Forest College Lake Forest		•							•	•	
Lewis University Romeoville		•		•	•				•	•	AF
Loyola University of Chicago Chicago		•			•	•	•		•	•	A N
MacMurray College Jacksonville		•		•	•				•	•	
Mallinckrodt College Wilmette		•			•					•	
McKendree College Lebanon		•			•				•	•	AF
Midwest College of Engineering Lombard					•					•	
Millikin University Decatur	•				•					•	

	External Degrees	Work-Study	Correspondence Courses	Life Experience	Proficiency Exams	Co-op Programs	Federal Co-op	Guaranteed Tuition	Accelerated Degrees	Advanced Placement	ROTC
Monmouth College Monmouth		•			•				•	•	
Moody Bible Institute Chicago					•					•	
Mundelein College Chicago		•		•	•	•	•		•	•	
National College of Education Evanston		•		•	•				•		
North Central College Naperville		•			•	•			•	•	AF
Northeastern Illinois University Chicago	•	•		•	•	•			•	•	AF
Northern Illinois University DeKalb		•			•	•	•		•	•	A AF
North Park College Chicago		•			•	•			•	•	N AF
Northwestern University Evanston		•				•	•		•	•	N AF
Olivet Nazarene College Kankakee		•			•	•			•	•	
Parks College of St. Louis Univ. Cahokia		•			•		•		•	•	AF
Principia College Esah					•	•			•	•	
Quincy College Quincy		•		•	•			•	•	•	
Rockford College Rockford		•			•				•	•	
Roosevelt University Chicago	•	•	•	•	•		•		•		
Rosary College River Forest		•		•	•		•		•	•	
Saint Xavier College Chicago		•		•	•				•	•	AF
School of the Art Institute of Chicago		•			•	•			•		
Shimer College Waukegan		•			•				•		
Southern Illinois University Carbondale	•	•		•	•	•	•		•	•	A AF

	External Degrees	Work-Study	Correspondence Courses	Life Experience	Proficiency Exams	Co-op Programs	Federal Co-op	Guaranteed Tuition	Accelerated Degrees	Advanced Placement	ROTC
Southern Illinois University Edwardsville		•			•	•	•			•	AF
Spertus College of Judaica Chicago		•			•				•	•	
Trinity Christian College Palos Heights		•			•				•	•	
Trinity College Deerfield		•			•	•				•	
University of Chicago		•					•		•	•	N AF
University of Illinois/Chicago		•			•	•	•		•	•	A N AF
University of Illinois/Urbana-Champaign Urbana		•	•	•	•	•	•		•	•	A N AF
Vandercook College of Music Chicago		•							•		
Western Illinois University Macomb	•	•		•	•	•	•		•	•	A
Wheaton College Wheaton		•			•				•	•	A
INDIANA											
Anderson College Anderson		•			•				•	•	
Ball State University Muncie		•	•	•	•	•	•		•	•	A
Bethel College Mishawaka		•		•	•				•	•	N
Butler University Indianapolis		•			•	•			•	•	AF
Calumet College Whiting		•		•	•	•	•		•		
DePauw University Greencastle		•		•	•			•	•	•	AF
Earlham College Richmond		•			•	•			•	•	
Fort Wayne Bible College Fort Wayne		•		•	•				•		
Franklin College of Indiana Franklin		•			•				•	•	

	External Degrees	Work-Study	Correspondence Courses	Life Experience	Proficiency Exams	Co-op Programs	Federal Co-op	Guaranteed Tuition	Accelerated Degrees	Advanced Placement	ROTC
Goshen College Goshen		•		•	•	•			•	•	
Grace College Winona Lake		•			•				•	•	
Hanover College Hanover									•	•	
Huntington College Huntington		•			•				•	•	
Indiana Central University Indianapolis		•			•	•	•		•	•	
Indiana Institute of Technology Fort Wayne	•	•			•	•			•		
Indiana State University Terre Haute		•	•	•	•	•	•		•	•	AF
Indiana University Bloomington	•	•	•	•	•	•	•		•	•	A AF
Indiana University/Kokomo	•	•		•	•				•	•	
Indiana University/South Bend	•	•		•	•		•		•		N AF
Indiana University East Richmond	•	•		•	•				•	•	
Indiana University Northwest Gary	•	•			•	•	•		•	•	
Indiana University–Purdue University Fort Wayne	•	•			•				•	•	
Indiana University–Purdue University Indianapolis	•	•		•	•	•	•		•	•	A AF
Indiana University Southeast New Albany	•	•		•	•				•	•	A AF
Manchester College North Manchester		•			•	•			•	•	
Marian College Indianapolis		•		•	•	•			•	•	AF
Marion College Marion		•			•	•	•		•	•	
Martin Center College Indianapolis		•		•	•				•		
Oakland City College		•		•	•	•			•	•	

	External Degrees	Work-Study	Correspondence Courses	Life Experience	Proficiency Exams	Co-op Programs	Federal Co-op	Guaranteed Tuition	Accelerated Degrees	Advanced Placement	ROTC
Purdue University West Lafayette		•		•	•	•	•		•	•	A N AF
Purdue University–Calumet Hammond		•			•	•				•	
Purdue University–North Central Westville		•			•	•				•	
Rose-Hulman Institute of Technology Terre Haute		•			•			•	•	•	A AF
Saint Francis College Fort Wayne		•			•		•				
Saint Joseph's College Rensselaer		•			•	•			•	•	
Saint Mary-of-the-Woods College Saint Mary-of-the-Woods	•	•		•	•				•	•	
Saint Mary's College Notre Dame		•			•	•				•	N AF
Saint Meinrad College Saint Meinrad		•		•	•				•	•	
Taylor University Upland					•				•	•	
Tri-State University Angola		•			•	•	•				
University of Evansville	•	•		•	•	•	•		•	•	
University of Notre Dame		•							•	•	A N AF
University of Southern Indiana Evansville		•				•				•	
Valparaiso University Valparaiso		•			•	•	•		•	•	
Wabash College Crawfordsville					•				•	•	
IOWA											
Briar Cliff College Sioux City		•		•	•	•			•	•	
Buena Vista College Storm Lake		•		•	•				•	•	
Central University of Iowa Pella		•			•					•	

Kentucky

	External Degrees	Work-Study	Correspondence Courses	Life Experience	Proficiency Exams	Co-op Programs	Federal Co-op	Guaranteed Tuition	Accelerated Degrees	Advanced Placement	ROTC
dsville College / sville		•			•				•	•	
ollege of Kentucky		•			•					•	
and College / urg		•							•	•	A
entucky University		•	•		•	•	•		•	•	A AF
wn College / wn									•	•	AF
Christian College		•			•		•	•	•		
State University		•		•	•	•	•		•	•	A AF
Wesleyan College / ro		•			•	•			•	•	
d State University		•		•	•	•	•			•	A
tate University		•	•		•	•	•		•	•	A
Kentucky University / Heights		•			•	•			•	•	A AF
College		•			•				•	•	
University		•			•					•	AF
More College / Hills		•			•	•	•		•	•	AF
nia University		•			•				•	•	AF
ollege / le		•		•	•				•	•	
y of Kentucky		•	•		•	•	•		•		AF
y of Louisville		•		•	•	•	•		•	•	A AF
Kentucky University / Green		•	•		•	•			•	•	A AF

Iowa

	External Degrees	Work-Study	Correspondence Courses	Life Experience	Proficiency Exams	Co-op Programs	Federal Co-op	Guaranteed Tuition	Accelerated Degrees	Advanced Placement	ROTC
Clarke College Dubuque		•		•	•	•			•	•	
Coe College Cedar Rapids		•			•			•			
Cornell College Mount Vernon		•			•				•	•	
Divine Word College Epworth		•			•					•	
Dordt College Sioux Center		•									
Drake University Des Moines		•		•	•	•	•		•	•	A AF
Faith Baptists Bible College Ankeny					•						
Graceland College Lamoni		•			•						
Grand View College Des Moines		•			•				•	•	
Grinnell College Grinnell		•							•	•	
Iowa State University Ames	•	•			•	•	•		•	•	A N AF
Iowa Wesleyan College Mount Pleasant					•				•	•	
Loras College Dubuque		•			•	•			•	•	
Luther College Decorah		•			•				•		
Maharishi International University Fairfield		•			•						
Marycrest College Davenport		•		•	•						
Morningside College Sioux City		•			•				•		
Mount Mercy College Cedar Rapids		•		•	•			•			
Mount Saint Clare College Clinton		•		•	•	•			•		
Northwestern College Orange City				•	•				•	•	

	External Degrees	Work-Study	Correspondence Courses	Life Experience	Proficiency Exams	Co-op Programs	Federal Co-op	Guaranteed Tuition	Accelerated Degrees	Advanced Placement	ROTC
Open Bible College Des Moines		•			•						
St. Ambrose College Davenport		•	•	•	•	•			•	•	
Simpson College Indianola		•		•	•				•	•	
University of Dubuque		•		•	•				•	•	A
University of Iowa Iowa City		•	•	•	•	•			•	•	A AF
University of Northern Iowa Cedar Rapids	•	•	•	•	•	•			•	•	A
Upper Iowa University Fayette	•	•				•		•	•		
Vennard College University Park		•				•			•		
Wartburg College Waverly		•		•	•				•	•	
Westmar College Le Mars		•		•	•		•		•	•	
William Penn College Oskaloosa		•		•	•	•			•	•	
KANSAS											
Baker University Baldwin City		•		•	•				•	•	
Benedictine College Atchison		•			•	•			•	•	
Bethany College Lindsborg		•							•		
Bethel College North Newton		•	•	•					•	•	
Emporia State University Emporia		•		•	•				•	•	A
Fort Hays State University Hays		•							•	•	A
Friends Bible College Haviland		•							•		
Friends University Wichita		•	•						•	•	
Kansas Newman College Wichita	•	•		•	•	•			•	•	

	External Degrees	Work-Study	Correspondence Courses	Life Experience	Profi...
Kansas State University Manhattan	•	•		•	
Kansas Wesleyan Salina		•		•	
Marymount College of Kansas Salina		•		•	
McPherson College McPherson		•			
Mid-America Nazarene College Olathe		•			
Ottawa University		•			
Pittsburg State University		•			
Saint Mary College Leavenworth		•			
Saint Mary of the Plains College Dodge City		•		•	
Southwestern College Winfield		•		•	•
Sterling College Sterling					
Tabor College Hillsboro			•		
University of Kansas Lawrence		•	•		
Washburn University of Topeka		•			
Wichita State University		•		•	•
KENTUCKY					
Alice Lloyd College Pippa Passes		•			
Asbury College Wilmore		•			
Bellarmine College Louisville		•			
Berea College Berea		•		•	
Brescia College Owensboro		•		•	

Campbe...
Campbe...

Centre...
Danville

Cumber...
Williams...

Eastern...
Richmon...

George...
Georgeto...

Kentuck...
Grayson

Kentuck...
Frankfor...

Kentuck...
Owensb...

Morehe...
Morehe...

Murray
Murray

Norther...
Highland...

Pikeville
Pikeville

Spalding...
Louisville...

Thomas...
Crestview...

Transylv...
Lexingto...

Union C...
Barbour...

Universi...
Lexingto...

Universi...

Western...
Bowling...

	External Degrees	Work-Study	Correspondence Courses	Life Experience	Proficiency Exams	Co-op Programs	Federal Co-op	Guaranteed Tuition	Accelerated Degrees	Advanced Placement	ROTC
LOUISIANA											
Centenary College of Louisiana Shreveport		•		•					•	•	A
Dillard University New Orleans		•		•			•		•	•	A N AF
Grambling State University Grambling		•			•	•				•	A AF
Louisiana College Pineville		•							•		
Louisiana State Univ. and A&M College Baton Rouge	•	•		•	•	•				•	A AF
Louisiana State University Shreveport		•		•	•	•	•		•	•	A N
Louisiana Tech University Ruston		•		•	•	•				•	AF
Loyola University New Orleans		•		•			•		•	•	A N AF
McNeese State University Lake Charles		•		•	•				•	•	A
Nicholls State University Thibodaux		•		•	•				•	•	A
Northeast Louisiana University Monroe		•		•					•	•	A
Northwestern State University of Louisiana Natchitoches		•		•					•	•	A
Our Lady of Holy Cross College New Orleans		•	•	•	•					•	AF
Saint Joseph Seminary College St. Benedict		•		•					•	•	
Southeastern Louisiana University Hammond		•	•	•	•	•	•		•	•	A
Southern University and A&M College Baton Rouge					•		•			•	A N AF
Southern University in New Orleans					•		•			•	AF
Tulane University New Orleans		•		•			•		•	•	A N AF

	External Degrees	Work-Study	Correspondence Courses	Life Experience	Proficiency Exams	Co-op Programs	Federal Co-op	Guaranteed Tuition	Accelerated Degrees	Advanced Placement	ROTC
Tulane University/Newcomb College New Orleans					•				•	•	
University of New Orleans		•				•	•				A N AF
University of Southwestern Louisiana Lafayette		•			•		•		•	•	AF
Xavier University of Louisiana New Orleans		•			•	•	•			•	N AF
MAINE											
Bates College Lewiston		•							•	•	
Bowdoin College Brunswick		•							•	•	
Colby College Waterville		•							•	•	
College of the Atlantic Bar Harbor		•			•	•				•	
Husson College Bangor		•			•	•		•		•	AF
Maine Maritime Academy Castine		•		•	•					•	N
Portland School of Art		•		•						•	
Saint Joseph's College North Windham	•	•		•	•	•				•	
Thomas College Waterville		•			•	•			•	•	
Unity College Unity		•			•	•	•	•	•	•	
University of Maine/Farmington		•			•	•			•	•	
University of Maine/Fort Kent		•			•	•				•	
University of Maine/Machias		•		•	•	•			•	•	
University of Maine/Orono		•			•	•	•		•	•	A N AF
University of Maine/Presque Isle		•		•	•	•			•	•	
University of New England Biddeford		•		•	•	•			•	•	

	External Degrees	Work-Study	Correspondence Courses	Life Experience	Proficiency Exams	Co-op Programs	Federal Co-op	Guaranteed Tuition	Accelerated Degrees	Advanced Placement	ROTC
University of Southern Maine Gorham		•		•	•					•	A AF
Westbrook College Portland		•		•	•					•	
MARYLAND											
Baltimore Hebrew College				•	•	•			•		
Bowie State College Bowie		•		•	•	•	•		•	•	A AF
Capitol Institute of Technology Kensington		•		•	•	•	•		•	•	
College of Notre Dame of Maryland Baltimore		•		•	•		•		•	•	
Columbia Union College Takoma Park	•	•		•	•	•	•		•	•	
Coppin State College Baltimore		•			•	•	•		•		
Frostburg State College Frostburg		•			•		•			•	A
Goucher College Towson		•		•	•		•		•	•	
Hood College Frederick		•		•	•				•	•	
Johns Hopkins University Baltimore		•					•	•	•	•	A AF
Loyola College Baltimore		•			•		•		•	•	A AF
Maryland Institute College of Art Baltimore		•		•	•				•	•	
Morgan State University Baltimore		•				•	•				A
Mount Saint Mary's College Emmitsburg		•		•	•	•	•	•	•	•	A
St. Mary's College of Maryland St Mary's City		•			•	•	•		•	•	
Salisbury State College Salisbury		•			•	•	•		•	•	A

	External Degrees	Work-Study	Correspondence Courses	Life Experience	Proficiency Exams	Co-op Programs	Federal Co-op	Guaranteed Tuition	Accelerated Degrees	Advanced Placement	ROTC
Towson State University Baltimore		•			•	•	•		•	•	AF
University of Maryland/College Park	•	•			•	•	•		•	•	AF
University of Maryland/Baltimore County Catonsville		•				•	•		•		
University of Maryland/Eastern Shore Princess Anne		•			•	•	•		•		
Washington Bible College Lanham		•			•				•	•	
Washington College Chestertown		•			•				•	•	AF
Western Maryland College Westminster		•			•		•		•	•	A AF
MASSACHUSETTS											
American International College Springfield		•			•			•	•	•	AF
Amherst College Amherst		•								•	AF
Anna Maria College Paxton		•		•	•				•	•	N AF
Assumption College Worcester		•		•	•					•	N AF
Atlantic Union College South Lancaster	•	•		•	•		•			•	
Babson College Babson Park		•		•	•				•	•	
Bentley College Waltham		•					•	•	•		AF
Berklee College of Music Boston		•			•				•	•	
Berkshire Christian College Lenox		•		•	•	•				•	
Boston College Chestnut Hill		•						•	•	•	
Boston Conservatory of Music		•								•	
Boston University		•			•	•	•	•	•	•	A N AF

	External Degrees	Work-Study	Correspondence Courses	Life Experience	Proficiency Exams	Co-op Programs	Federal Co-op	Guaranteed Tuition	Accelerated Degrees	Advanced Placement	ROTC
Bradford College Bradford		•		•	•				•	•	
Brandeis University Waltham		•					•			•	
Bridgewater State College Bridgewater		•			•					•	
Central New England College Worcester		•		•	•	•	•		•	•	N AF
Clark University Worcester		•		•	•			•	•	•	N AF
College of the Holy Cross Worcester		•						•	•	•	N AF
Curry College Milton		•		•	•	•					
Eastern Nazarene College Quincy		•		•	•				•	•	
Elms College Chicopee		•		•	•				•	•	
Emerson College Boston		•			•					•	
Emmanuel College Boston		•		•	•				•	•	
Fitchburg State College Fitchburg	•	•			•				•	•	A
Framingham State College Framingham	•	•			•					•	
Gordon College Wenham		•			•	•		•	•	•	AF
Hampshire College Amherst		•	•						•		
Harvard and Radcliffe Colleges Cambridge		•				•	•	•	•	N AF
Hebrew College Brookline		•							•		
Hellenic College Brookline		•		•	•					•	
Lesley College Cambridge		•			•					•	
Massachusetts College of Art Boston		•		•	•	•				•	

	External Degrees	Work-Study	Correspondence Courses	Life Experience	Proficiency Exams	Co-op Programs	Federal Co-op	Guaranteed Tuition	Accelerated Degrees	Advanced Placement	ROTC
Mass. College of Pharmacy and Allied Health Sciences Boston		•		•	•					•	
Massachusetts Institute of Technology Cambridge		•				•	•		•	•	A N AF
Massachusetts Maritime Academy Buzzards Bay		•				•					
Merrimack College North Andover		•		•	•		•			•	
Mount Holyoke College South Hadley		•						•	•	•	AF
Mount Ida College Newton Centre		•		•	•	•				•	
New England Conservatory of Music Boston		•			•						
Nichols College Dudley		•		•	•						
North Adams State College North Adams		•		•	•				•	•	
Northeastern University Boston		•		•	•	•	•		•	•	A AF
Pine Manor College Chestnut Hill		•		•	•				•		
Regis College Weston		•									
St. Hyacinth College and Seminary Granby					•					•	
Saint John's Seminary Brighton		•								•	
Salem State College Salem		•		•	•	•				•	A AF
School of the Museum of Fine Arts Boston		•									
Simmons College Boston		•		•	•	•			•	•	
Simon's Rock of Bard College Great Barrington		•		•	•				•		

	External Degrees	Work-Study	Correspondence Courses	Life Experience	Proficiency Exams	Co-op Programs	Federal Co-op	Guaranteed Tuition	Accelerated Degrees	Advanced Placement	ROTC
Smith College Northampton		•						•	•	•	AF
Southeastern Massachusetts University North Dartmouth		•		•	•				•	•	
Springfield College Springfield		•			•	•			•	•	AF
Stonehill College North Easton		•			•				•	•	A
Suffolk University Boston		•			•				•	•	A
Swain School of Design New Bedford		•									
Tufts University Medford		•					•	•	•	•	N AF
University of Lowell		•			•	•	•			•	AF
University of Massachusetts/Amherst	•	•		•	•	•	•		•	•	A AF
University of Massachusetts/Boston		•		•	•	•	•		•		
Wellesley College Wellesley		•						•	•	•	N AF
Wentworth Institute of Technology Boston	•	•		•	•	•	•		•		
Western New England College Springfield		•			•				•	•	A AF
Westfield State College Westfield		•			•	•			•	•	A
Wheaton College Norton		•							•	•	
Wheelock College Boston		•		•	•					•	
Williams College Williamstown		•							•	•	
Worcester Polytechnic Institute Worcester		•				•	•		•	•	A N AF
Worcester State College Worcester		•		•	•					•	N AF

	External Degrees	Work-Study	Correspondence Courses	Life Experience	Proficiency Exams	Co-op Programs	Federal Co-op	Guaranteed Tuition	Accelerated Degrees	Advanced Placement	ROTC
MICHIGAN											
Adrian College Adrian		•		•	•					•	
Albion College Albion		•			•	•			•	•	
Alma College Alma		•			•				•	•	
Andrews University Berrien Springs		•		•	•	•			•	•	
Aquinas College Grand Rapids	•	•		•	•	•	•	•	•	•	
Calvin College Grand Rapids		•		•	•			•	•	•	
Central Michigan University Mount Pleasant	•	•	•	•	•	•			•	•	A
Cleary College Ypsilanti		•		•	•	•			•	•	
Concordia College Ann Arbor		•		•	•				•	•	AF
Davenport College of Business Grand Rapids	•	•		•		•			•		
Detroit College of Business Dearborn		•		•	•	•			•		
Eastern Michigan University Ypsilanti		•	•		•	•	•		•	•	A N AF
Ferris State College Grand Rapids	•	•		•	•	•	•		•	•	
General Motors Institute Flint		•			•	•			•	•	
Grace Bible College Grand Rapids		•		•						•	
Grand Rapids Baptist College		•		•						•	
Grand Valley State Colleges Allendale		•		•	•	•			•	•	
Hillsdale College Hillsdale				•					•	•	
Hope College Holland		•		•					•	•	
John Wesley College Owosso								•			
Jordan College Cedar Springs		•		•	•	•			•	•	

	External Degrees	Work-Study	Correspondence Courses	Life Experience	Proficiency Exams	Co-op Programs	Federal Co-op	Guaranteed Tuition	Accelerated Degrees	Advanced Placement	ROTC
Kalamazoo College Kalamazoo		•				•				•	
Lake Superior State College Sault Ste. Marie		•			•				•	•	
Lawrence Institute of Technology Southfield		•			•	•	•			•	AF
Madonna College Livonia		•		•	•	•	•		•	•	
Marygrove College Detroit		•		•	•	•	•		•	•	
Mercy College of Detroit	•	•			•	•	•			•	
Michigan Christian College Rochester		•			•				•	•	
Michigan State University East Lansing		•			•	•				•	A AF
Northern Michigan University Marquette		•			•				•	•	A
Northwood Institute Midland	•	•		•	•	•			•	•	
Oakland University Rochester		•			•	•	•		•	•	
Olivet College Olivet		•		•	•	•		•	•	•	
Reformed Bible College Grand Rapids		•			•	•			•		
Sacred Heart Seminary College Detroit		•		•	•					•	
Saginaw Valley State College University Center		•			•	•	•		•	•	
St. Mary's College Orchard Lake		•		•	•	•	•		•	•	
Siena Heights College Adrian	•	•		•	•				•	•	
Spring Arbor College Spring Arbor	•	•		•	•				•	•	
University of Detroit		•			•	•	•		•	•	A
University of Michigan Ann Arbor		•	•		•	•			•	•	A N AF
University of Michigan/Dearborn		•			•				•	•	AF
University of Michigan/Flint		•			•				•	•	

	External Degrees	Work-Study	Correspondence Courses	Life Experience	Proficiency Exams	Co-op Programs	Federal Co-op	Guaranteed Tuition	Accelerated Degrees	Advanced Placement	ROTC
Wayne State University Detroit	•	•			•	•	•		•	•	AF
Western Michigan University Kalamazoo	•	•	•		•	•	•		•	•	A
MINNESOTA											
Augsburg College Minneapolis		•		•	•	•	•			•	N AF
Bemidji State University Bemidji	•	•		•	•	•	•		•	•	A
Bethel College St. Paul		•			•	•				•	N AF
Carleton College Northfield		•						•	•	•	
College of Saint Benedict Saint Joseph		•		•	•				•		
College of St. Catherine St. Paul		•		•	•		•		•	•	AF
College of St. Scholastica Duluth	•	•		•	•				•	•	AF
College of Saint Teresa Winona		•		•	•				•		
College of St. Thomas St. Paul		•			•	•	•			•	N AF
Concordia College Moorhead		•			•	•			•	•	AF
Concordia College St. Paul		•		•	•				•	•	N AF
Dr. Martin Luther College New Ulm					•				•		
Gustavus Adolphus College St. Peter		•			•	•	•		•		
Hamline University St. Paul		•			•	•			•	•	AF
Macalester College St. Paul										•	N AF
Mankato State University Mankato		•			•	•	•		•	•	A
Minneapolis College of Art & Design Minneapolis	•				•				•		

	External Degrees	Work-Study	Correspondence Courses	Life Experience	Proficiency Exams	Co-op Programs	Federal Co-op	Guaranteed Tuition	Accelerated Degrees	Advanced Placement	ROTC
Minnesota Bible College Rochester					•						
Moorhead State University	•	•		•	•	•	•			•	AF
North Central Bible College Minneapolis		•			•						
Northwestern College Roseville		•			•					•	AF
St. Cloud State University St. Cloud		•		•	•	•	•		•	•	
Saint John's University Collegeville		•				•				•	A
Saint Mary's College Winona		•		•	•				•	•	
St. Olaf College Northfield		•			•				•	•	
St. Paul Bible College Bible College		•						•		•	
Southwest State University Marshall	•	•		•	•	•			•		
University of Minnesota/Duluth		•			•				•	•	AF
University of Minnesota/Morris	•	•			•	•			•	•	
University of Minnesota/Twin Cities Minneapolis	•	•	•			•	•		•		A N AF
Winona State University Winona	•	•		•	•	•			•	•	A
MISSISSIPPI											
Alcorn State University Lorman				•	•	•	•		•		A
Belhaven College Jackson		•			•				•		
Blue Mountain College Blue Mountain		•			•				•		
Delta State University Cleveland		•			•	•	•		•	•	A AF
Jackson State University Jackson		•			•	•	•		•	•	A
Millsaps College Jackson		•		•	•		•		•		

	External Degrees	Work-Study	Correspondence Courses	Life Experience	Proficiency Exams	Co-op Programs	Federal Co-op	Guaranteed Tuition	Accelerated Degrees	Advanced Placement	ROTC
Mississippi College Clinton		•				•			•		
Mississippi State University Mississippi State			•	•	•	•	•		•	•	A AF
Mississippi University for Women Columbus					•	•	•		•	•	AF
Mississippi Valley State University Itta Bena					•	•					AF
Rust College Holly Springs		•				•	•				
Tougaloo College Tougaloo		•			•	•	•		•		
University of Mississippi University		•	•		•	•			•	•	A N AF
University of Southern Mississippi Hattiesburg		•	•		•	•	•		•	•	A AF
William Carey College Hattiesburg		•			•		•		•	•	AF
MISSOURI											
Avila College Kansas City		•		•	•	•		•	•		
Calvary Bible College Kansas City					•				•	•	
Central Bible College Springfield		•			•	•			•		
Central Methodist College Fayette		•			•				•	•	
Central Missouri State University Warrensburg		•		•	•	•	•		•	•	A
Clayton University Clayton	•			•	•						
Columbia College Columbia		•		•	•				•		N AF
Conception Seminary College Conception		•			•					•	
Culver-Stockton College Canton		•	•	•	•				•	•	

	External Degrees	Work-Study	Correspondence Courses	Life Experience	Proficiency Exams	Co-op Programs	Federal Co-op	Guaranteed Tuition	Accelerated Degrees	Advanced Placement	ROTC
Drury College Springfield		•			•				•	•	
Evangel College Springfield					•				•	•	
Fontbonne College St. Louis		•		•	•	•			•	•	
Hannibal-LaGrange College Hannibal		•		•	•	•			•	•	
Harris-Stowe State College St. Louis					•		•		•		AF
Kansas City Art Institute		•			•	•				•	
Lincoln University Jefferson City		•			•	•	•		•		A N
Lindenwood College St. Charles	•	•		•	•	•		•	•	•	
Maryville College–St. Louis		•		•	•	•			•	•	
Missouri Baptist College St. Louis					•				•		
Missouri Southern State College Joplin		•			•				•		A
Missouri Valley College Marshall		•		•	•	•			•	•	
Missouri Western State College St. Joseph		•			•		•		•		A
Northeast Missouri State University Kirksville		•			•	•	•		•	•	A
Northwest Missouri State University Maryville		•			•	•		•	•	•	
Park College Parkville		•		•	•	•			•		
Rockhurst College Kansas City		•			•	•	•		•	•	
St. Louis College of Pharmacy		•			•					•	
Saint Louis Conservatory of Music		•			•	•				•	
Saint Louis University		•		•	•		•		•	•	AF
School of the Ozarks Point Lookout		•			•	•			•		

	External Degrees	Work-Study	Correspondence Courses	Life Experience	Proficiency Exams	Co-op Programs	Federal Co-op	Guaranteed Tuition	Accelerated Degrees	Advanced Placement	ROTC
Southeast Missouri State University Cape Girardeau					•	•	•		•	•	AF
Southwest Baptist University Bolivar		•		•	•				•	•	
Southwest Missouri State University Springfield		•			•	•	•		•	•	A
Stephens College Columbia	•	•		•	•				•	•	N AF
Tarkio College Tarkio	•	•		•	•	•		•	•	•	
University of Missouri/Columbia		•	•	•	•	•	•		•	•	A N AF
University of Missouri/Kansas City	•	•		•	•	•	•		•	•	
University of Missouri/Rolla		•				•	•			•	A AF
University of Missouri/St. Louis		•			•	•	•			•	A AF
Washington University St. Louis		•			•	•		•	•	•	A AF
Webster University St. Louis		•		•	•				•	•	
Westminster College Fulton		•			•					•	A
William Jewel College Liberty		•			•	•			•	•	
William Woods College Fulton		•			•				•	•	N AF
MONTANA											
Carroll College Helena		•			•	•			•	•	
College of Great Falls		•			•	•			•		
Eastern Montana College Billings			•		•				•	•	A
Montana College of Mineral Science and Technology Butte		•			•	•	•		•		
Montana State University Bozeman		•			•	•				•	A AF

	External Degrees	Work-Study	Correspondence Courses	Life Experience	Proficiency Exams	Co-op Programs	Federal Co-op	Guaranteed Tuition	Accelerated Degrees	Advanced Placement	ROTC
Northern Montana College Havre		•			•	•	•		•		
Rocky Mountain College Billings		•		•	•	•			•	•	
University of Montana Missoula		•			•	•	•		•	•	A
Western Montana College Dillon		•			•	•			•	•	
NEBRASKA											
Bellevue College Bellevue		•		•	•		•		•		AF
Chadron State College Chadron	•	•		•	•	•	•		•		
College of Saint Mary Omaha		•		•	•					•	AF
Concordia Teachers College Seward		•			•				•	•	AF
Creighton University Omaha		•				•	•	•	•	•	A AF
Dana College Crete		•		•	•	•			•	•	
Hastings College Hastings		•		•	•	•	•		•	•	
Kearney State College Kearney		•			•	•			•	•	A
Midland Lutheran College Fremont		•			•				•	•	
Nebraska Wesleyan University Lincoln	•	•		•	•				•	•	N AF
Peru State College Peru		•			•	•			•		
Union College Lincoln		•			•	•			•	•	
University of Nebraska/Lincoln		•	•	•	•	•	•		•	•	A N AF
University of Nebraska/Omaha		•			•	•		•	•	•	A AF
Wayne State College Wayne		•			•		•		•	•	

	External Degrees	Work-Study	Correspondence Courses	Life Experience	Proficiency Exams	Co-op Programs	Federal Co-op	Guaranteed Tuition	Accelerated Degrees	Advanced Placement	ROTC
NEVADA											
Old College Reno	•			•	•	•			•	•	
Sierra Nevada College Incline Village		•		•	•				•		
University of Nevada/Las Vegas		•			•		•		•	•	A
University of Nevada/Reno		•	•		•	•	•			•	A
NEW HAMPSHIRE											
Colby-Sawyer College New London		•		•	•				•	•	AF
Daniel Webster College Nashua		•		•	•	•			•	•	AF
Dartmouth College Hanover		•					•	•		•	A
Franklin Pierce College Rindge		•		•	•				•	•	
Hawthorne College Antrim	•	•		•	•				•	•	
Keene State College Keene		•			•	•			•	•	AF
New England College Henniker		•			•					•	AF
New Hampshire College Manchester		•			•	•	•			•	AF
Notre Dame College Manchester		•		•	•				•	•	AF
Plymouth State College Plymouth		•		•	•				•	•	AF
Rivier College Nashua		•			•					•	AF
St. Anselm's College Manchester		•			•					•	AF
University of New Hampshire Durham		•			•	•	•		•	•	A AF
NEW JERSEY											
Bloomfield College		•		•	•				•	•	
Caldwell College		•			•	•			•	•	

	External Degrees	Work-Study	Correspondence Courses	Life Experience	Proficiency Exams	Co-op Programs	Federal Co-op	Guaranteed Tuition	Accelerated Degrees	Advanced Placement	ROTC
Centenary College Hackettstown		•		•	•				•	•	
College of Saint Elizabeth Convent Station		•			•				•	•	
Don Bosco College Newton		•			•			•	•		
Drew University Madison		•			•	•		•	•	•	
Fairleigh Dickinson Univ./Florham-Madison Madison		•			•					•	
Fairleigh Dickinson Univ./Rutherford		•		•	•	•	•			•	
Fairleigh Dickinson Univ./Teaneck-Hackensack Teaneck		•			•					•	AF
Felician College Lodi		•			•					•	
Georgian Court College Lakewood		•		•	•	•				•	
Glassboro State College Glassboro		•			•		•		•		
Jersey City State College Jersey City		•			•	•	•		•	•	A AF
Kean College of New Jersey Union		•		•		•	•		•		AF
Monmouth College West Long Branch		•		•	•		•		•	•	A AF
Montclair State College Upper Montclair		•		•	•	•	•		•	•	AF
New Jersey Institute of Technology Newark		•			•	•	•		•	•	AF
Northeast Bible College Essex Falls		•		•	•				•	•	
Princeton University Princeton		•			•		•		•	•	A AF
Ramapo College of New Jersey Mahwah		•		•	•	•	•		•	•	
Rider College Lawrenceville		•			•	•		•	•	•	A AF

	External Degrees	Work-Study	Correspondence Courses	Life Experience	Proficiency Exams	Co-op Programs	Federal Co-op	Guaranteed Tuition	Accelerated Degrees	Advanced Placement	ROTC
Rutgers University/Camden College Camden		•								•	AF
Rutgers University/New Brunswick		•			•	•	•			•	A AF
Saint Peter's College Jersey City	•	•		•	•	•	•		•	•	A AF
Seton Hall University South Orange		•			•	•	•		•	•	A AF
Stevens Institute of Technology Hoboken		•			•				•		AF
Stockton State College Pomona		•			•	•	•	•			
Trenton State College Trenton		•			•	•	•		•	•	AF
Upsala College East Orange		•		•	•				•	•	AF
Westminster Choir College Princeton		•								•	
William Paterson College of New Jersey Wayne		•			•		•		•	•	AF
NEW MEXICO											
College of Santa Fe	•	•		•	•	•	•			•	
College of the Southwest Hobbs				•	•				•	•	
Eastern New Mexico State University Portales		•		•	•	•	•		•	•	A
New Mexico Highlands University Las Vegas		•			•	•	•			•	A
New Mexico Institute of Mining and Technology Socorro		•				•	•			•	A
New Mexico State University Las Cruces		•			•	•	•		•	•	A AF
St. John's College Santa Fe		•									
University of New Mexico Albuquerque		•	•		•	•	•		•	•	N AF

	External Degrees	Work-Study	Correspondence Courses	Life Experience	Proficiency Exams	Co-op Programs	Federal Co-op	Guaranteed Tuition	Accelerated Degrees	Advanced Placement	ROTC
Western New Mexico Silver City		•		•	•	•			•	•	
NEW YORK											
Adelphi University Garden City		•		•	•				•	•	AF
Albany College of Pharmacy of Union University Albany		•		•	•					•	AF
Alfred University Alfred		•			•	•	•		•	•	AF
Bard College Annandale	•	•							•	•	
Barnard College New York		•							•	•	
Boricua College New York	•	•		•	•				•	•	
Canisius College Buffalo		•		•	•		•		•	•	
CUNY/Bernard Baruch College New York		•		•	•		•		•	•	
CUNY/Brooklyn College Brooklyn		•			•				•	•	
CUNY/City College New York		•		•	•	•	•		•	•	
CUNY/College of Staten Island		•		•	•				•	•	
CUNY/Herbert H. Lehman College Bronx		•		•	•	•	•		•	•	
CUNY/Hunter College New York		•			•	•	•		•	•	
CUNY/John Jay College of Criminal Justice New York		•		•	•	•	•			•	A
CUNY/Medgar Evers College Brooklyn		•			•	•	•				
CUNY/Queens College Flushing		•		•	•				•	•	
CUNY/York College Jamaica		•			•	•	•			•	

	External Degrees	Work-Study	Correspondence Courses	Life Experience	Proficiency Exams	Co-op Programs	Federal Co-op	Guaranteed Tuition	Accelerated Degrees	Advanced Placement	ROTC
Clarkson University Potsdam		•		•	•				•	•	A AF
Colgate University Hamilton		•		•	•			•	•	•	
College for Human Services New York					•				•		
College of Insurance New York		•	•	•	•						
College of Mount Saint Vincent Riverdale		•	•	•	•				•	•	AF
College of New Rochelle	•	•	•	•				•	•	•	
College of Saint Rose Albany		•	•	•					•	•	N AF
Columbia University New York		•					•			•	AF
Concordia College Bronxville		•							•	•	
Cooper Union for the Advancement of Science and Art New York		•		•	•					•	
Cornell University Ithaca		•				•	•	•	•	•	A N AF
Daemen College Amherst		•	•	•	•	•					
Dominican College Orangeburg		•							•	•	
Dowling College Oakdale		•	•	•	•	•			•	•	AF
D'Youville College Buffalo		•							•		
Elmira College Elmira		•		•					•	•	
Fashion Institute of Technology New York		•	•	•	•						
Fordham University Bronx		•	•	•	•				•	•	A N
Friends World College Huntington	•	•	•	•					•		
Hamilton College Clinton		•							•	•	

	External Degrees	Work-Study	Correspondence Courses	Life Experience	Proficiency Exams	Co-op Programs	Federal Co-op	Guaranteed Tuition	Accelerated Degrees	Advanced Placement	ROTC
Hartwick College Oneonta		•		•	•				•	•	
Hobart College Geneva		•		•	•				•	•	AF
Hofstra University Hempstead		•		•	•				•	•	A
Houghton College Houghton		•			•	•			•	•	
Iona College New Rochelle		•		•	•	•			•	•	
Ithaca College Ithaca		•			•				•	•	N AF
Juilliard School New York		•							•		
Keuka College Keuka Park		•		•	•	•			•	•	AF
King's College Briarcliff Manor		•			•				•		
Le Moyne College Syracuse		•			•		•		•	•	AF
Long Island Univ./Brooklyn Center Brooklyn		•		•	•	•			•	•	AF
Long Island Univ./C. W. Post Campus Greenvale		•		•	•	•	•		•	•	AF
Long Island Univ./Southampton College Southampton		•		•	•	•	•		•	•	
Manhattan College Riverdale		•			•	•			•	•	AF
Manhattan School of Music New York		•			•						
Manhattanville College Purchase		•			•	•			•	•	
Mannes College of Music New York		•						•	•		
Marist College Poughkeepsie		•		•	•	•	•		•		
Marymount College Tarrytown		•		•	•	•			•	•	

	External Degrees	Work-Study	Correspondence Courses	Life Experience	Proficiency Exams	Co-op Programs	Federal Co-op	Guaranteed Tuition	Accelerated Degrees	Advanced Placement	ROTC
Marymount Manhattan College New York		•		•	•				•	•	
Medaille College Buffalo		•		•	•				•	•	
Mercy College Dobbs Ferry		•		•	•				•	•	AF
Molloy College Rockville Centre		•		•	•	•			•	•	AF
Mount Saint Mary College Newburgh		•		•	•				•	•	
Nazareth College of Rochester Rochester		•							•	•	N AF
New School for Social Research New York		•			•				•	•	AF
New York Institute of Technology Old Westbury	•	•		•	•	•			•	•	AF
New York University		•		•	•	•			•	•	
Niagara University Niagara University		•		•	•	•	•		•	•	A
Nyack College Nyack		•									
Pace University New York		•		•	•	•		•	•	•	AF
Pace University/College of White Plains		•		•	•	•			•	•	
Pace University/Pleasantville-Briarcliff Pleasantville		•		•	•	•			•	•	
Parsons School of Design New York		•							•		
Polytechnic University Brooklyn		•				•	•		•		A AF
Pratt University Brooklyn		•	•	•	•	•	•		•		
Rensselaer Polytechnic Institute Troy		•				•	•		•	•	A N AF
Roberts Wesleyan College Rochester		•			•					•	AF

	External Degrees	Work-Study	Correspondence Courses	Life Experience	Proficiency Exams	Co-op Programs	Federal Co-op	Guaranteed Tuition	Accelerated Degrees	Advanced Placement	ROTC
Rochester Institute of Technology		•		•	•	•	•			•	A N AF
Russell Sage College Troy		•		•	•					•	N AF
St. Bonaventure University St. Bonaventure		•							•	•	A
St. Francis College Brooklyn		•		•	•	•			•	•	AF
St. John Fisher College Rochester		•		•	•				•	•	N AF
St. John's University Jamaica		•		•	•				•	•	A
St. Joseph's College Brooklyn		•		•	•				•		
St. Joseph's College/Suffolk Patchogue		•			•					•	AF
St. Lawrence University Canton		•			•				•	•	A AF
Siena College Loudonville		•			•				•	•	A N AF
Skidmore College Saratoga Springs	•	•		•	•				•	•	N AF
State University of NY/Albany		•			•				•	•	A N AF
State University of NY/Binghamton		•			•		•		•		
State University of NY/Buffalo		•		•	•	•	•		•		
State University of NY/Stony Brook		•			•					•	AF
SUNY College/Brockport	•	•		•	•	•			•	•	A N AF
SUNY College/Buffalo		•		•	•	•			•		
SUNY College/Cortland		•			•	•	•			•	A N AF
SUNY College/Fredonia		•		•	•	•	•		•	•	A
SUNY College/Geneseo		•			•				•	•	N AF
SUNY College/New Paltz		•		•	•	•	•		•	•	
SUNY College/Old Westbury		•		•	•						AF
SUNY College/Oneonta		•		•	•				•		
SUNY College/Oswego		•		•	•	•				•	A

	External Degrees	Work-Study	Correspondence Courses	Life Experience	Proficiency Exams	Co-op Programs	Federal Co-op	Guaranteed Tuition	Accelerated Degrees	Advanced Placement	ROTC
SUNY College/Plattsburgh		•			•	•	•			•	
SUNY College/Potsdam		•			•	•				•	AF
SUNY College/Purchase		•			•					•	
SUNY College of Technology Utica		•			•	•			•		
SUNY Empire State College Saratoga Springs	•		•	•	•					•	
SUNY Maritime College Bronx		•		•						•	N
Syracuse University Syracuse	•	•				•	•	•	•	•	A AF
Touro College New York		•		•	•				•		
Union College Schenectady		•							•	•	N AF
University of Rochester		•				•	•		•	•	N AF
Utica College of Syracuse University Utica		•		•	•		•		•	•	AF
Vassar College Poughkeepsie		•				•			•	•	
Wadhams Hall Seminary-College Ogdensburg		•			•				•		
Wagner College Staten Island				•	•				•	•	AF
Webb Institute of Naval Architecture Glen Cove						•					
Wells College Aurora		•							•	•	AF
William Smith College Geneva		•		•	•				•	•	
Yeshiva University New York		•		•					•		
NORTH CAROLINA											
Appalachian State University Boone		•	•		•				•	•	A
Atlantic Christian College Wilson		•			•	•	•		•	•	

	External Degrees	Work-Study	Correspondence Courses	Life Experience	Proficiency Exams	Co-op Programs	Federal Co-op	Guaranteed Tuition	Accelerated Degrees	Advanced Placement	ROTC
Barber-Scotia College Concord		•			•	•			•		AF
Belmont Abbey College Belmont		•	•	•		•			•	•	AF
Bennett College Greensboro					•		•		•	•	AF
Campbell University Buies Creek		•			•	•	•		•	•	A
Catawba College Salisbury		•	•	•					•	•	
Davidson College Davidson		•			•				•	•	A AF
Duke University Durham		•					•	•	•	•	A N AF
East Carolina University Greenville		•			•	•	•		•	•	A AF
Elizabeth City State University Elizabeth City	•	•			•	•	•				
Elon College Elon College		•			•	•	•		•		A
Fayetteville State University Fayetteville		•	•	•	•	•	•		•	•	AF
Gardner-Webb College Boiling Springs		•			•				•	•	
Greensboro College Greensboro		•			•				•	•	AF
Guilford College Greensboro		•			•				•	•	AF
High Point College High Point		•	•	•	•					•	AF
Johnson C. Smith University Charlotte		•				•	•		•	•	AF
Lenoir-Rhyne College Hickory		•	•	•	•	•			•	•	
Livingstone College Salisbury		•			•	•	•				
Mars Hill College Mars Hill	•	•		•	•	•			•	•	
Meredith College Raleigh		•		•	•	•	•		•	•	AF
Methodist College Fayetteville		•			•			•	•	•	

	External Degrees	Work-Study	Correspondence Courses	Life Experience	Proficiency Exams	Co-op Programs	Federal Co-op	Guaranteed Tuition	Accelerated Degrees	Advanced Placement	ROTC
Mount Olive College Mount Olive					•	•				•	
North Carolina A&T State University Greensboro		•			•	•	•			•	A AF
North Carolina Central University Durham		•			•	•	•			•	N AF
North Carolina School of the Arts Winston-Salem		•			•						
North Carolina State University/Raleigh		•	•		•	•	•		•	•	A N AF
North Carolina Wesleyan College Rocky Mount	•	•			•	•			•		
Pembroke State University Pembroke		•			•	•	•		•		AF
Pfeiffer College Misenheimer		•			•	•			•	•	
Piedmont Bible College Winston-Salem					•				•		
Queens College Charlotte		•			•				•	•	AF
Sacred Heart College Belmont		•		•	•			•	•	•	AF
St. Andrews Presbyterian College Laurinburg		•			•				•	•	
Saint Augustine's College Raleigh		•				•			•		A AF
Salem College Winston-Salem	•	•		•	•				•		
Shaw University Raleigh				•	•						AF
University of North Carolina/Asheville		•	•		•				•	•	
University of North Carolina/Chapel Hill		•	•		•	•			•	•	N AF
University of North Carolina/Charlotte		•			•	•	•		•	•	A AF
University of North Carolina/Greensboro		•	•		•	•			•	•	AF

	External Degrees	Work-Study	Correspondence Courses	Life Experience	Proficiency Exams	Co-op Programs	Federal Co-op	Guaranteed Tuition	Accelerated Degrees	Advanced Placement	ROTC
University of North Carolina/Wilmington		•			•	•	•		•	•	A
Wake Forest University Winston-Salem		•			•				•	•	A
Warren Wilson College Swannanoa		•		•	•	•			•	•	
Western Carolina University Cullowhee		•	•	•	•	•	•		•	•	A
Wingate College Wingate		•			•				•	•	AF
Winston-Salem State University Winston-Salem		•	•		•	•	•		•		
Winthrop College Rock Hill		•			•				•		AF
NORTH DAKOTA											
Dickinson State College Dickinson				•	•	•			•		
Jamestown College Jamestown		•			•				•	•	
Mary College Bismarck	•	•		•	•	•			•	•	
Mayville State College Mayville		•				•	•				
Minot State College Minot		•			•	•			•		
North Dakota State University Bottineau		•			•	•					
North Dakota State University Fargo		•		•	•	•	•		•	•	A AF
Northwest Bible College Minot		•			•	•			•		
University of North Dakota Grand Forks		•	•		•	•	•		•	•	A
Valley City State College Valley City		•		•	•	•			•		
OHIO											
Antioch College Yellow Springs	•	•		•	•	•	•			•	AF

	External Degrees	Work-Study	Correspondence Courses	Life Experience	Proficiency Exams	Co-op Programs	Federal Co-op	Guaranteed Tuition	Accelerated Degrees	Advanced Placement	ROTC
Ashland College Ashland		•			•	•			•	•	AF
Baldwin-Wallace College Berea		•		•	•	•	•		•	•	AF
Bluffton College Bluffton		•			•				•	•	
Borreomeo College of Ohio Wickliffe		•			•				•	•	
Bowling Green State University Bowling Green		•		•	•	•	•		•	•	A AF
Capital University Columbus		•		•	•	•			•	•	N AF
Case Western Reserve University Cleveland		•				•	•	•	•	•	AF
Cedarville College Cedarville					•				•	•	AF
Central State University Wilberforce		•				•	•			•	A AF
Cleveland Institute of Art		•			•				•	•	
Cleveland Institute of Music		•		•	•				•	•	
Cleveland State University		•			•	•	•		•	•	
College of Mount St. Joseph Mount St. Joseph		•		•	•	•			•	•	AF
College of Wooster		•							•		
Defiance College Defiance		•		•	•	•	•		•	•	AF
Denison University Granville		•		•	•	•			•		
Dyke College Cleveland	•	•				•	•		•	•	
Findlay College Findlay		•		•	•				•	•	AF
Franklin University Columbus		•		•	•		•		•		A AF
Heidelberg College Tiffin		•		•	•				•	•	AF
Hiram College Hiram					•				•	•	
John Carroll University University Heights		•			•	•	•		•	•	A

	External Degrees	Work-Study	Correspondence Courses	Life Experience	Proficiency Exams	Co-op Programs	Federal Co-op	Guaranteed Tuition	Accelerated Degrees	Advanced Placement	ROTC
of Oklahoma	•	•	•		•	•	•			•	•	A N AF
cience and Arts of		•			•				•	•	
of Tulsa		•				•			•	•	A
Christian College		•			•					•	
College		•								•	AF
regon State College	•	•		•	•	•	•		•	•	A
x College		•			•	•			•	•	
Clark College		•							•	•	
ollege	•	•	•	•	•				•	•	
st College for Learning		•		•	•					•	
Christian College		•			•	•				•	
nstitute of		•		•		•				•	A
tate University		•			•	•	•			•	A AF
niversity		•			•					•	
State University		•	•	•	•	•			•	•	A AF
llege		•			•				•		
Oregon State		•		•	•					•	
y of Oregon		•			•	•	•			•	A A
y of Portland		•			•	•	•		•	•	A

	External Degrees	Work-Study	Correspondence Courses	Life Experience	Proficiency Exams	Co-op Programs	Federal Co-op	Guaranteed Tuition	Accelerated Degrees	Advanced Placement	ROTC
Kent State University Kent		•			•	•	•	•	•	•	A AF
Kenyon College Gambier		•						•	•	•	
Lake Erie College Painesville	•	•		•	•	•				•	
Malone College Canton		•		•	•	•	•			•	
Marietta College Marietta		•			•			•		•	
Miami University Oxford		•		•	•	•				•	N AF
Mount Union College Alliance	•	•		•	•				•	•	AF
Mount Vernon Nazarene College Mount Vernon		•			•				•	•	
Muskingum College New Concord		•		•	•				•	•	
Notre Dame College of Ohio Cleveland		•		•	•	•					
Oberlin College		•						•	•		
Ohio Dominican College Columbus		•		•	•	•				•	N AF
Ohio Northern University Ada		•			•				•	•	AF
Ohio State University/Columbus		•		•	•	•	•		•	•	A N AF
Ohio State University/Lima		•		•	•	•	•		•	•	A N AF
Ohio State University/Mansfield		•		•	•	•	•		•	•	A N AF
Ohio State University/Marion		•		•	•	•	•		•	•	A N AF
Ohio State University/Newark		•		•	•	•	•		•	•	A N AF
Ohio University Athens	•	•	•	•	•					•	A AF
Ohio University/Belmont	•	•		•	•				•	•	A AF
Ohio University/Chillicothe		•		•	•	•			•	•	A AF

	External Degrees	Work-Study	Correspondence Courses	Life Experience	Proficiency Exams	Co-op Programs	Federal Co-op	Guaranteed Tuition	Accelerated Degrees	Advanced Placement	ROTC
Ohio University/Zanesville	•	•		•	•	•			•	•	
Ohio Wesleyan University Delaware		•							•	•	AF
Otterbein College Westerville		•		•	•	•				•	N AF
Pontifical College Josephinum Columbus		•						•			
Rio Grande College Rio Grande		•		•	•				•	•	A
Tiffin University Tiffin		•		•	•						
Union for Experimenting Colleges and Universities Cincinnati	•			•	•						
University of Akron		•		•	•	•			•	•	A AF
University of Cincinnati		•	•	•	•	•			•	•	A AF
University of Dayton		•		•	•	•			•	•	A AF
University of Steubenville		•				•					
University of Toledo		•		•	•				•	•	A AF
Urbana University		•		•	•				•	•	AF
Ursuline College Pepper Pike	•	•		•	•	•			•	•	
Walsh College North Canton		•		•					•	•	
Wilberforce University Wilberforce		•		•	•	•	•				AF
Wilmington College Wilmington		•		•	•	•	•			•	AF
Wittenberg University Springfield		•							•	•	AF
Wright State University Dayton		•		•	•	•			•	•	A AF
Xavier University Cincinnati		•		•		•	•		•	•	A AF
Youngstown State University Youngstown		•		•	•				•	•	A

	External Degrees	Work-Study	Correspondence Courses	Life
OKLAHOMA				
Bartlesville Wesleyan College Bartlesville		•	•	
Bethany Nazarene College Bethany		•		
Cameron University Lawton		•		
Central State University Edmond		•		
East Central University Ada		•		
Hillsdale Free Will Baptist College Moore		•		
Langston University Langston		•		
Northeastern Oklahoma State Univ. Tahlequah				
Northwestern Oklahoma State Univ. Alva		•		
Oklahoma Baptist University Shawnee		•		
Oklahoma Christian College Oklahoma City		•		
Oklahoma City University	•		•	
Oklahoma Panhandle State Univ. Goodwell		•		
Oklahoma State University Stillwater		•	•	•
Oral Roberts University Tulsa		•		•
Phillips University Enid		•		
Southeastern Oklahoma State Univ. Durant		•		•
Southwestern Oklahoma State Univ. Weatherford		•		

	External Degrees	Work-Study	Correspondence Courses	Life
University Norman				
Univ. of S Oklahoma Chickasha				
University				
OREGON				
Columbia Portland				
Concordi Portland				
Eastern O La Grande				
George F Newberg				
Lewis and Portland				
Linfield C McMinnvi				
Marylhur Lifelong Marylhurs				
Northwe Eugene				
Oregon Technolo Klamath				
Oregon S Corvallis				
Pacific U Forest Gr				
Portland Portland				
Reed Co Portland				
Southern College Ashland				
Universi Eugene				
Universi				

	External Degrees	Work-Study	Correspondence Courses	Life Experience	Proficiency Exams	Co-op Programs	Federal Co-op	Guaranteed Tuition	Accelerated Degrees	Advanced Placement	ROTC
Warner Pacific College Portland		•		•	•					•	AF
Western Baptist College Salem		•		•	•	•					
Western Oregon State College Monmouth		•			•				•	•	AF
Willamette University Salem		•							•	•	AF
PENNSYLVANIA											
Academy of the New Church Bryn Athyn									•	•	
Albright College Reading		•		•	•				•	•	
Allegheny College Meadville		•			•			•	•	•	
Allentown College of St. Francis de Sales Center Valley		•		•					•	•	AF
Alliance College Cambridge Springs		•		•	•	•			•	•	
Alvernia College Reading		•		•	•	•			•	•	
Baptist Bible College of Pennsylvania Clarks Summit				•	•				•	•	
Beaver College Glenside		•			•	•	•		•	•	
Bloomsburg University Bloomsburg		•		•	•	•			•	•	AF
Bryn Mawr College Bryn Mawr		•							•	•	N AF
Bucknell University Lewisburg		•			•				•	•	A
Cabrini College Radnor		•		•	•	•			•	•	
California University of Pennsylvania California		•		•	•	•			•	•	A
Carlow College Pittsburgh		•			•				•	•	AF

	External Degrees	Work-Study	Correspondence Courses	Life Experience	Proficiency Exams	Co-op Programs	Federal Co-op	Guaranteed Tuition	Accelerated Degrees	Advanced Placement	ROTC
Carnegie-Mellon University Pittsburgh		•				•	•		•	•	A N AF
Cedar Crest College Allentown		•		•	•	•			•	•	AF
Chatham College Pittsburgh		•		•	•				•	•	AF
Chestnut Hill College Philadelphia		•		•	•	•	•		•	•	
Cheyney University Cheyney		•		•		•	•		•	•	AF
Clarion University Clarion		•		•	•	•	•		•	•	A
College Misericordia Dallas		•		•	•	•			•	•	AF
Combs College of Music Philadelphia		•		•	•				•	•	
Delaware Valley College of Science and Agriculture Doylestown		•		•	•	•	•		•		
Dickinson College Carlisle		•							•	•	A
Drexel University Philadelphia		•		•	•	•			•	•	A N AF
Duquesne University Pittsburgh		•		•	•	•			•	•	A AF
Eastern College St. Davids		•		•	•	•			•	•	AF
East Stroudsburg University East Stroudsburg		•			•					•	A AF
Edinboro University Edinboro		•		•	•		•		•	•	
Elizabethtown College Elizabethtown	•	•		•	•				•	•	
Franklin and Marshall College Lancaster		•			•		•		•	•	
Gannon University Erie	•	•			•	•			•	•	A
Geneva College Beaver Falls		•		•	•		•		•	•	
Gettysburg College Gettysburg		•			•				•	•	A

	External Degrees	Work-Study	Correspondence Courses	Life Experience	Proficiency Exams	Co-op Programs	Federal Co-op	Guaranteed Tuition	Accelerated Degrees	Advanced Placement	ROTC
Gratz College Philadelphia				•					•		
Grove City College Grove City					•				•	•	AF
Gwynedd-Mercy College Gwynedd Valley	•			•	•				•		
Hahnemann University Philadelphia	•				•	•					
Haverford College Haverford	•				•				•	•	AF
Holy Family College Philadelphia	•			•	•	•			•		
Immaculata College Immaculata	•				•				•		
Indiana University of Pennsylvania Indiana	•			•	•	•	•		•	•	A
Juniata College Huntingdon	•								•	•	
King's College Wilkes-Barre	•			•	•	•				•	AF
Kutztown State College Kutztown	•				•	•			•	•	AF
Lafayette College Easton	•						•		•	•	A AF
Lancaster Bible College Lancaster	•				•			•	•		
La Roche College Pittsburgh	•			•	•	•			•	•	AF
La Salle University Philadelphia	•				•	•	•		•	•	A N AF
Lebanon Valley College Annville	•			•	•				•		
Lehigh University Bethlehem	•				•	•			•	•	A AF
Lincoln University Lincoln University	•				•	•	•		•	•	AF
Lock Haven University Lock Haven	•				•	•			•	•	A
Lycoming College Williamsport	•			•	•				•	•	

	External Degrees	Work-Study	Correspondence Courses	Life Experience	Proficiency Exams	Co-op Programs	Federal Co-op	Guaranteed Tuition	Accelerated Degrees	Advanced Placement	ROTC
Mansfield University Mansfield		•		•	•				•	•	A
Marywood College Scranton	•	•		•	•	•			•		AF
Mercyhurst College Erie		•		•	•	•	•		•	•	
Messiah College Grantham					•	•	•				
Millersville University Millersville					•	•	•		•	•	A
Moore College of Art Philadelphia		•				•			•		
Moravian College Bethlehem		•			•				•	•	AF
Muhlenberg College Allentown		•			•				•	•	AF
Neumann College Aston		•		•	•				•	•	
Pennsylvania State University University Park	•	•	•		•	•	•		•	•	A N AF
Philadelphia Colleges of the Arts		•			•				•	•	
Philadelphia College of Bible Langhorne		•			•				•	•	
Philadelphia College of Pharmacy and Science		•								•	
Philadelphia College of Textiles and Science		•			•	•	•			•	
Point Park College Pittsburgh		•		•	•	•	•		•	•	AF
Robert Morris College Coraopolis		•		•	•	•	•		•	•	AF
Rosemont College		•		•	•	•			•	•	
Saint Charles Borromeo Seminary Philadelphia		•								•	
Saint Francis College Loretto		•			•				•	•	
Saint Joseph's University Philadelphia		•		•	•	•	•		•	•	N AF
Saint Vincent College Latrobe		•		•	•	•				•	AF

	External Degrees	Work-Study	Correspondence Courses	Life Experience	Proficiency Exams	Co-op Programs	Federal Co-op	Guaranteed Tuition	Accelerated Degrees	Advanced Placement	ROTC
Seton Hill College Greensburg		•		•	•				•	•	
Shippensburg University		•	•	•	•		•		•	•	A
Slippery Rock University		•		•	•	•			•	•	A AF
Spring Garden College Chestnut Hill		•	•	•				•	•	•	
Susquehanna University Selinsgrove		•	•	•	•				•	•	
Swarthmore College Swarthmore		•							•	•	N AF
Temple University Philadelphia		•	•	•	•	•			•	•	A N AF
Thiel College Greenville		•		•	•				•		
United Wesleyan College Allentown		•							•		
University of Pennsylvania Philadelphia		•				•	•		•	•	A N AF
University of Pittsburgh	•	•		•			•			•	A AF
University of Pittsburgh/Bradford		•		•					•	•	
University of Pittsburgh/Greensburg		•		•					•	•	
University of Pittsburgh/Johnstown		•		•							
University of Scranton		•	•	•		•			•	•	A AF
Ursinus College Collegeville		•		•					•	•	
Valley Forge Christian College Phoenixville		•	•	•					•	•	
Villa Maria College Erie		•		•	•	•			•		
Villanova University Villanova		•		•			•			•	N AF
Washington and Jefferson College Washington		•		•					•	•	A
Waynesburg College Waynesburg		•	•	•	•	•			•	•	

	External Degrees	Work-Study	Correspondence Courses	Life Experience	Proficiency Exams	Co-op Programs	Federal Co-op	Guaranteed Tuition	Accelerated Degrees	Advanced Placement	ROTC
West Chester University West Chester		•			•				•	•	AF
Westminster College New Wilmington		•	•					•	•	•	
Widener University Chester		•			•	•	•		•	•	A AF
Wilkes College Wilkes-Barre	•	•		•	•	•	•		•	•	AF
Wilson College Chambersburg		•		•	•		•		•	•	
York College of Pennsylvania York		•			•		•		•	•	
RHODE ISLAND											
Brown University Providence		•					•		•	•	
Bryant College Smithfield		•			•		•		•	•	A
Johnson and Wales College Providence		•		•	•	•			•	•	
New England Institute of Technology Providence		•		•	•	•		•			
Providence College Providence		•					•			•	A
Rhode Island College Providence		•		•	•	•			•	•	A
Rhode Island School of Design Providence		•							•		
Roger Williams College Bristol	•	•		•	•	•	•		•	•	
Salve Regina/Newport College Newport		•		•	•	•			•	•	
University of Rhode Island Kingston		•			•		•		•	•	A
SOUTH CAROLINA											
Baptist College at Charleston					•				•	•	
Benedict College Columbia		•			•	•				•	A AF
Central Wesleyan College Central		•			•				•	•	AF

	External Degrees	Work-Study	Correspondence Courses	Life Experience	Proficiency Exams	Co-op Programs	Federal Co-op	Guaranteed Tuition	Accelerated Degrees	Advanced Placement	ROTC
The Citadel Charleston					•					•	A N AF
Clemson University Clemson		•			•	•	•		•	•	A AF
Coker College Hartsville		•			•	•			•	•	
College of Charleston Charleston		•			•	•	•		•	•	
Columbia Bible College Columbia		•			•				•	•	
Columbia College Columbia		•		•	•				•	•	
Converse College Spartanburg		•		•	•				•	•	
Erskine College Due West		•			•	•			•	•	A
Francis Marion College Florence		•			•	•			•	•	A
Furman University Greenville		•				•	•		•	•	A
Lander College Greenwood		•			•	•	•		•	•	
Limestone College Gaffney		•			•				•	•	
Morris College Sumter		•				•	•			•	
Newberry College Newberry		•			•	•		•	•	•	
Presbyterian College Clinton		•			•				•	•	A
South Carolina State College Orangeburg		•				•	•			•	A
University of South Carolina Columbia	•	•	•		•	•	•		•	•	A N AF
University of South Carolina/Aiken		•			•	•			•	•	
University of South Carolina/Spartanburg Spartanburg		•			•				•	•	
University of South Carolina/Coastal Carolina College Conway		•			•				•	•	

	External Degrees	Work-Study	Correspondence Courses	Life Experience	Proficiency Exams	Co-op Programs	Federal Co-op	Guaranteed Tuition	Accelerated Degrees	Advanced Placement	ROTC
Voorhees College Denmark		•									
Winthrop College Rock Hill		•			•	•	•		•	•	
Wofford College Spartanburg		•			•	•	•		•	•	A
SOUTH DAKOTA											
Augustana College Sioux Falls		•		•	•	•	•		•	•	
Black Hills State College Spearfish		•			•				•	•	A
Dakota State College Madison		•		•	•	•			•		
Dakota Wesleyan University Mitchell		•		•	•				•		
Mount Marty College Yankton		•		•	•	•			•		
National College Rapid City		•		•	•	•			•	•	
Northern State College Aberdeen		•			•	•	•		•	•	A
Sinte Gleska College Rosebud		•									
Sioux Falls College Sioux Falls		•		•	•	•			•	•	
South Dakota School of Mines and Technology Rapid City		•			•	•				•	A
South Dakota State University Brookings		•			•	•	•		•	•	A AF
University of South Dakota Vermillion	•	•	•		•	•			•	•	A
TENNESSEE											
Austin Peay State University Clarksville		•			•		•		•	•	A
Belmont College Nashville		•	•		•				•	•	N AF
Bethel College McKenzie		•	•	•					•	•	

	External Degrees	Work-Study	Correspondence Courses	Life Experience	Proficiency Exams	Co-op Programs	Federal Co-op	Guaranteed Tuition	Accelerated Degrees	Advanced Placement	ROTC
Bryan College Dayton		•			•					•	
Christian Brothers College Memphis		•			•				•	•	AF
Cumberland University Lebanon		•		•	•					•	
David Lipscomb College Nashville		•			•				•	•	N AF
East Tennessee State University Johnson City		•			•	•	•		•	•	A
Fisk University Nashville		•			•	•	•			•	N AF
Freed-Hardeman College Henderson		•			•	•			•	•	
Free Will Baptist Bible College Nashville		•			•					•	
Johnson Bible College Knoxville		•			•				•	•	
King College Bristol		•			•						
Knoxville College Knoxville		•				•				•	AF
Lambuth College Jackson		•			•		•		•	•	
Lane College Jackson		•				•	•				
Lee College Cleveland		•			•	•	•			•	
LeMoyne-Owen College Memphis					•	•	•			•	AF
Lincoln Memorial University Harrogate		•		•	•	•			•	•	
Maryville College		•			•					•	
Memphis College of Art Memphis		•		•	•			•	•	•	
Memphis State University Memphis		•		•	•	•	•		•	•	A N AF
Middle Tennessee State University Murfreesboro		•		•	•	•	•		•	•	A AF
Milligan College Milligan College		•							•	•	

	External Degrees	Work-Study	Correspondence Courses	Life Experience	Proficiency Exams	Co-op Programs	Federal Co-op	Guaranteed Tuition	Accelerated Degrees	Advanced Placement	ROTC
Rhodes College Memphis		•							•	•	AF
Southern College of Seventh-Day Adventists Collegedale		•			•				•	•	
Tennessee State University Nashville						•	•		•		N AF
Tennessee Technological University Cookeville		•			•	•	•		•	•	A
Tennessee Temple University Chattanooga		•			•	•			•		
Tennessee Wesleyan College Athens					•				•	•	
Trevecca Nazarene College Nashville		•	•	•		•			•	•	N AF
Tusculum College Greeneville	•	•	•	•					•	•	
Union University Jackson					•				•	•	
University of Tennessee/Chattanooga		•	•	•	•	•	•		•	•	A
University of Tennessee/Knoxville		•	•	•	•	•	•		•	•	A AF
University of Tennessee/Martin	•	•	•	•	•	•	•		•	•	A
University of the South Sewanee		•							•	•	
Vanderbilt University Nashville		•							•	•	A N AF
TEXAS											
Abilene Christian University Abilene		•		•	•				•	•	
Angelo State University San Angelo		•			•		•		•	•	AF
Austin College Sherman		•			•				•	•	
Baylor University Waco		•			•	•			•	•	AF
Bishop College Dallas			•	•	•	•			•	•	A

	External Degrees	Work-Study	Correspondence Courses	Life Experience	Proficiency Exams	Co-op Programs	Federal Co-op	Guaranteed Tuition	Accelerated Degrees	Advanced Placement	ROTC
Concordia Lutheran College Austin		•			•						AF
Dallas Baptist University Dallas		•		•	•		•			•	
Dallas Christian College Dallas		•			•			•		•	
Devry Institute of Technology Irving		•				•			•		
East Texas Baptist College Marshall	•	•		•	•				•	•	
East Texas State University Commerce		•		•	•	•	•		•	•	AF
Hardin-Simmons University Abilene		•			•				•	•	A
Houston Baptist University Houston		•			•				•	•	N
Howard Payne University Brownwood		•			•						
Huston-Tillotson College Austin		•		•	•						
Incarnate Word College San Antonio		•		•	•	•			•	•	
Jarvis Christian College Hawkins				•	•				•		
Lamar University Beaumont				•	•	•			•	•	A
LeTourneau College Longview		•		•	•				•		
Lubbock Christian College Lubbock					•		•		•	•	AF
McMurry College Abilene		•							•	•	
Midwestern State University Wichita Falls		•		•	•				•	•	A
North Texas State University Denton		•			•	•	•		•	•	AF
Our Lady of the Lake University San Antonio		•		•	•		•		•	•	
Pan American University Edinburg		•				•	•		•		A

	External Degrees	Work-Study	Correspondence Courses	Life Experience	Proficiency Exams	Co-op Programs	Federal Co-op	Guaranteed Tuition	Accelerated Degrees	Advanced Placement	ROTC
Paul Quinn College Waco					•	•	•				AF
Prairie View A&M University Prairie View	•	•			•	•	•		•	•	A N
Rice University Houston		•			•		•		•	•	N
St. Edward's University Austin	•	•			•	•			•	•	N AF
St. Mary's University of San Antonio		•	•	•	•	•	•		•	•	A
Sam Houston State University Huntsville		•			•	•			•		A
Schreiner College Kerrville		•	•	•	•				•		
Southern Methodist University Dallas		•			•	•	•	•	•	•	AF
Southwestern Adventist College Keene	•	•	•	•		•			•		
Southwestern University Georgetown		•		•					•	•	
Southwest Texas State University San Marcos		•	•	•			•		•	•	AF
Stephen F. Austin State University Nacogdoches		•	•				•		•	•	A
Sul Ross State University Alpine		•		•							
Tarleton State University Stephenville		•								•	A
Texas A&I University Kingsville		•	•	•			•		•	•	A
Texas A&M University College Station		•			•	•	•		•	•	A N AF
Texas A&M University/Galveston		•			•		•		•		
Texas Christian University Fort Worth		•	•	•			•		•	•	A AF
Texas College Tyler		•									A
Texas Lutheran College Seguin		•			•	•	•		•	•	AF

	External Degrees	Work-Study	Correspondence Courses	Life Experience	Proficiency Exams	Co-op Programs	Federal Co-op	Guaranteed Tuition	Accelerated Degrees	Advanced Placement	ROTC
Texas Southern University Houston				•		•	•				N
Texas Tech University Lubbock	•		•		•		•		•	•	A N AF
Texas Wesleyan College Fort Worth		•			•				•	•	AF
Texas Women's University Denton		•			•	•	•		•	•	A AF
Trinity University San Antonio		•			•		•		•	•	A
University of Dallas Irving		•		•	•				•	•	AF
University of Houston Houston		•			•	•	•		•	•	A N
University of Mary Hardin–Baylor Belton		•			•	•			•	•	AF
University of St. Thomas Houston		•			•	•				•	N
University of Texas/Arlington		•		•	•	•	•		•	•	A AF
University of Texas/Austin		•	•		•	•	•			•	A N AF
University of Texas/El Paso		•			•	•	•		•	•	A AF
University of Texas/San Antonio		•			•	•	•		•	•	A AF
Wayland Baptist University Plainview	•						•	•			
West Texas State University Canyon					•	•				•	A
Wiley College Marshall		•			•						
UTAH											
Brigham Young University Provo	•		•		•	•	•		•	•	A AF
Southern Utah State College Cedar City		•			•	•	•		•	•	
University of Utah Salt Lake City		•	•		•	•	•		•	•	A N AF

	External Degrees	Work-Study	Correspondence Courses	Life Experience	Proficiency Exams	Co-op Programs	Federal Co-op	Guaranteed Tuition	Accelerated Degrees	Advanced Placement	ROTC
Utah State University Logan		•	•		•	•	•		•	•	A AF
Weber State College Ogden		•		•	•	•	•		•	•	A N AF
Westminster College Salt Lake City		•		•	•	•			•	•	N AF
VERMONT											
Bennington College Bennington		•				•				•	N
Burlington College South Burlington		•		•	•	•			•	•	
Castleton State College Castleton	•	•		•	•	•			•		
College of St. Joseph Rutland		•		•					•		
Goddard College Plainfield	•	•		•	•	•			•		
Green Mountain College Poultney		•			•	•			•	•	
Johnson State College Johnson	•	•			•	•			•		
Lyndon State College Lyndonville		•		•	•	•				•	AF
Marlboro College Marlboro		•			•	•			•	•	
Middlebury College Middlebury		•							•		
Norwich University Northfield		•		•	•	•			•	•	A N AF
Saint Michael's College Winooski		•			•					•	AF
Southern Vermont College Bennington		•		•	•	•			•		
Trinity College Burlington	•	•		•	•					•	AF
University of Vermont Burlington		•			•	•	•			•	A AF
Vermont College of Norwich University Montpelier	•	•		•	•	•			•	•	

	External Degrees	Work-Study	Correspondence Courses	Life Experience	Proficiency Exams	Co-op Programs	Federal Co-op	Guaranteed Tuition	Accelerated Degrees	Advanced Placement	ROTC
VIRGINIA											
Averett College Danville		•		•	•			•	•	•	
Bluefield College Bluefield		•			•				•	•	
Bridgewater College Bridgewater		•					•		•	•	
Christopher Newport College Newport News		•			•		•		•	•	A
Clinch Valley College of University of Virginia Wise		•				•		•			
College of William & Mary Williamsburg		•				•				•	A
Eastern Mennonite College Harrisonburg		•			•				•		
Emory and Henry College Emory		•		•	•				•		
Ferrum College Ferrum		•			•				•		
George Mason University Fairfax		•		•	•	•	•		•	•	A AF
Hampden-Sydney College Hampden-Sydney		•					•		•	•	
Hampton University Hampton		•			•	•	•			•	A N
Hollins College Roanoke		•							•	•	
James Madison University Harrisonburg		•		•	•		•		•	•	A
Liberty University Lynchburg		•		•	•	•			•	•	
Longwood College Farmville		•			•				•	•	A
Lynchburg College Lynchburg		•		•	•				•	•	A
Mary Baldwin College Staunton	•	•		•	•				•	•	
Marymount University Arlington		•		•	•	•			•	•	
Mary Washington College Fredericksburg		•		•	•		•		•	•	

	External Degrees	Work-Study	Correspondence Courses	Life Experience	Proficiency Exams	Co-op Programs	Federal Co-op	Guaranteed Tuition	Accelerated Degrees	Advanced Placement	ROTC
Norfolk State University Norfolk		•			•	•	•		•	•	A N
Old Dominion University Norfolk		•			•	•	•		•	•	A N
Radford University Radford		•			•						
Randolph-Macon College Ashland		•			•		•		•	•	
Randolph-Macon Women's College Lynchburg				•	•	•			•	•	
Roanoke College Salem		•							•	•	
Saint Paul's College Lawrenceville		•				•	•				
Shenandoah College & Conservatory Winchester		•			•				•	•	
Sweet Briar College Sweet Briar		•							•	•	
University of Richmond					•		•		•	•	A
University of Virginia Charlottesville		•					•		•	•	A N AF
Virginia Commonwealth University Richmond		•	•	•	•	•	•		•	•	
Virginia Intermont College Bristol		•		•	•				•		
Virginia Military Institute Lexington										•	A N AF
Virginia Polytech Institute and State University Blacksburg		•				•	•			•	A N AF
Virginia State University Petersburg		•	•	•	•	•		•			A
Virginia Union University Richmond		•				•	•				
Virginia Wesleyan College Norfolk		•	•	•			•		•	•	
Washington and Lee University Lexington		•					•			•	A

WASHINGTON

	External Degrees	Work-Study	Correspondence Courses	Life Experience	Proficiency Exams	Co-op Programs	Federal Co-op	Guaranteed Tuition	Accelerated Degrees	Advanced Placement	ROTC
Central Washington University Ellensburg		•				•	•		•	•	A
Cornish Institute Seattle		•		•	•					•	
Eastern Washington University Cheney		•		•		•	•		•	•	A
Evergreen State College Olympia		•		•	•						
Gonzaga University Spokane		•		•	•	•	•		•	•	A
Griffin College Seattle		•			•				•		
Northwest College of the Assemblies of God Kirkland		•		•	•				•		
Pacific Lutheran University Tacoma		•		•	•	•	•		•	•	AF
Saint Martin's College Olympia				•	•		•			•	AF
Seattle Pacific University Seattle		•		•	•	•				•	N AF
Seattle University		•					•		•	•	A N AF
University of Puget Sound Tacoma		•			•	•	•			•	AF
University of Washington Seattle		•	•			•	•			•	A N AF
Walla Walla College College Place		•				•	•		•		
Washington State University Pullman			•		•	•	•		•	•	A N AF
Western Washington University Bellingham	•	•	•		•		•		•		
Whitman College Walla Walla		•							•	•	
Whitworth College Spokane		•			•			•		•	

	External Degrees	Work-Study	Correspondence Courses	Life Experience	Proficiency Exams	Co-op Programs	Federal Co-op	Guaranteed Tuition	Accelerated Degrees	Advanced Placement	ROTC
WEST VIRGINIA											
Alderson-Broaddus College Philippi		•		•	•				•	•	
Bethany College Bethany		•	•	•					•	•	
Bluefield State College Bluefield	•	•			•		•		•		
Concord College Athens	•	•			•				•	•	
Davis and Elkins College Elkins		•	•	•					•		
Fairmont State College Fairmont	•	•	•	•		•			•	•	AF
Glenville State College Glenville	•	•	•	•		•			•		
Marshall University Huntington		•	•	•	•	•			•	•	A
Salem College Salem		•			•				•	•	
Shepherd College Shepherdstown	•	•			•				•	•	AF
University of Charleston		•	•	•	•	•	•	•	•	•	
West Liberty State College West Liberty	•	•		•	•				•	•	
West Virginia Institute of Technology Montgomery			•	•	•	•	•		•	•	
West Virginia State College Institute	•	•	•	•	•				•	•	A
West Virginia University Morgantown	•	•	•	•	•	•			•	•	A AF
West Virginia Wesleyan College Buckhannon		•	•	•	•				•	•	
Wheeling College Wheeling		•	•	•	•					•	
WISCONSIN											
Alverno College Milwaukee		•	•	•	•				•	•	
Beloit College Beloit		•			•					•	

	External Degrees	Work-Study	Correspondence Courses	Life Experience	Proficiency Exams	Co-op Programs	Federal Co-op	Guaranteed Tuition	Accelerated Degrees	Advanced Placement	ROTC
Cardinal Stritch College Milwaukee		•		•	•				•	•	
Carroll College Waukesha		•			•				•	•	
Carthage College Kenosha		•			•	•			•	•	
Concordia College Mequon		•			•			•		•	
Edgewood College Madison		•		•	•					•	
Lakeland College Sheboygan	•	•			•				•	•	
Lawrence University Appleton		•								•	
Marian College of Fond du Lac		•		•	•				•	•	
Marquette University Milwaukee		•			•	•	•	•		•	A N AF
Milwaukee Institute of Art and Design		•		•		•					
Mount Mary College Milwaukee		•		•	•				•	•	
Mount Senario College Ladysmith	•	•		•	•	•		•	•	•	
Northland College Ashland		•			•	•	•	•	•	•	
Ripon College Ripon		•			•				•	•	A
St. Norbert College De Pere		•		•	•	•			•	•	A
Silver Lake College Manitowoc		•			•						
University of Wisconsin/Eau Claire		•			•	•				•	
University of Wisconsin/Green Bay	•	•		•	•		•		•	•	
University of Wisconsin/La Crosse		•		•	•	•	•		•	•	A
University of Wisconsin/Madison	•	•	•	•	•	•	•		•	•	A N AF
University of Wisconsin/Milwaukee		•		•	•	•	•		•	•	A N

	External Degrees	Work-Study	Correspondence Courses	Life Experience	Proficiency Exams	Co-op Programs	Federal Co-op	Guaranteed Tuition	Accelerated Degrees	Advanced Placement	ROTC
University of Wisconsin/Oshkosh		•		•	•	•	•		•	•	A
University of Wisconsin/Parkside Kenosha					•		•		•	•	
University of Wisconsin/Platteville	•	•		•	•	•	•		•	•	A
University of Wisconsin/River Falls		•			•	•	•		•	•	
University of Wisconsin/Stevens Point		•		•	•	•	•		•	•	A
University of Wisconsin/Stout Menomonie	•				•	•			•		
University of Wisconsin/Superior		•		•	•	•				•	AF
University of Wisconsin/Whitewater	•	•			•		•			•	A
WYOMING											
University of Wyoming Laramie		•	•		•		•			•	A AF
PUERTO RICO											
Catholic University of Puerto Rico Ponce		•					•		•	•	
Inter American University San Juan				•	•	•	•			•	AF
University of Puerto Rico Mayaguez		•				•	•			•	A AF
University of Puerto Rico Rio Piedras		•				•			•		A AF
University of the Sacred Heart Santurce		•					•		•	•	AF
GUAM											
University of Guam Mangilao		•		•			•		•		A

INDEX